"*Year of Fire Dragons* evokes all ⌐.⌐ ..e wonder of being in love as a young expat while capturing the true romance of Hong Kong. As you delight in Shannon Young's deftly written coming-of-age story, you might just find yourself falling for this fiery city where East meets West."

> – Jocelyn Eikenburg, Speaking of China

"Life's twists and turns are like the tail of a dragon, but this intrepid American millennial holds on tight to her dreams to carve out her place (creatively, financially and romantically) in Hong Kong – a world far from home. Shannon Young's delightful memoir shows us that true discoveries are made when we let go of who we think we are and embrace who we might become."

> – Leza Lowitz, author of *Here Comes The Sun: A Yogi's Journey of Adapting and Adopting in Japan*

"After moving halfway around the world for love, Shannon Young unexpectedly finds herself living alone in Hong Hong. One brave, adventurous step at a time, she finds her footing in her new city and in her own life."

> – Lisa McKay, author of *Love at the Speed of Email* and founder of Modern Love Long Distance

"Shannon's memoir was so inspiring because it shows that two people can live so far apart in the world and yet be so committed to love."

> – Jane Cornelius, author of *Baby and a Backpack*

YEAR OF FIRE DRAGONS

An American Woman's Story
of Coming of Age in Hong Kong

Shannon Young

BLACKSMITH BOOKS

This book is for my husband. Thank you for making me laugh, being my friend, and forgiving me when I set things on fire in the kitchen. Most of all, thank you for bringing me to Hong Kong. I love our life together, and wouldn't want it any other way.

Year of Fire Dragons
ISBN 978-988-13764-1-1

Published by Blacksmith Books
5th Floor, 24 Hollywood Road, Hong Kong
Tel: (+852) 2877 7899
www.blacksmithbooks.com

Also by Shannon Young:
• *The Art of Escalator Jumping*
• *Pay Off: How One Millennial Eliminated Nearly $80,000 in Student Debt in Less Than Five Years*
• *The Olympics Beat: A Spectator's Memoir of Beijing*
• *How Does One Dress to Buy Dragonfruit?: True Stories of Expat Women in Asia* (editor)

CONTENTS

ACKNOWLEDGEMENTS

I would like to thank the people who have been instrumental in the creation of this book.

For their company and encouragement: Betsy Cheung, Laura Cook, Suvi Lampila, Helen Innes, Amanda Tong, Kaitlin Trowbridge, Marie Sweetman, Willow Hewitt, Terri Chan, Rachel Marsh and everyone else who has come to Holly Brown to write on a Tuesday night.

For their online friendship and support: Susan Blumberg-Kason, Jocelyn Eikenburg, Lisa McKay, Leza Lowitz, Mel Ulm, Laura Besley, ML Awanohara, Tom Carter, Joyce Barnes, Julie Fritz, Ressie Ho, Ana Costa, Kaela Chow and everyone else who has read and commented on *A Kindle in Hong Kong* over the past four years.

For making my time at the school in Kowloon Bay so precious: Grace, Flora, Fung, Celine, Winnie, Sean, Candy, Hilda, Stella, Rita, Cherry, Olivia, Wing Man, Anderson, Joseph and of course, Alex.

For their advice on the publishing business: Kevin Conroy Scott, Xu Xi, Marshall Moore, Kelly Falconer, Mike Tsang and Susan Blumberg-Kason.

For reading many rough drafts and offering excellent feedback: Kaylee Peelen, Stephanie Barnoff, Whitney Galletly, Kaitlyn Godfrey, Chelsea Nieuwoudt, Hollie Ivany, and Ayden and Julie Young.

For being a first-rate critique partner and a boundless source of inspiration: Jane Cornelius.

For allowing me to share the letters she wrote during her time in Hong Kong: my grandmother, Donna Young.

For his confidence in this story and his work to make the book a reality: Pete Spurrier.

For the beautiful cover I can't stop staring at: Cara Wilson.

And finally, thank you to my family for your constant encouragement and belief in me, especially my parents, Ayden and Julie Young, and all my siblings. Thank you, also, to my in-laws for welcoming me into your family here in Hong Kong.

I

Fire Dragon

The fire dragon trundled toward me through the crowded street. Smoke curled from the incense sticks protruding from its long, thin body like thousands of spines on some mystical porcupine. Sweat poured down the face and back of every spectator. The fire dragon wound back and forth through the streets, faster and faster, dancing to the beat of drums. A wave of cheers rippled through the crowd each time it came near. The drums rattled the high-rises, the dragon danced, and the pavement shuddered under our feet.

This was the Mid-Autumn Festival in Hong Kong, a time to celebrate the moon goddess and her flight across the sky.

My flight wasn't like that of Chang'e, the goddess who escaped her lover in a blaze of luminescence. I was flying toward mine. His gravitational field had pulled me across the sea, drawn me to a distant isle of fire dragons and skyscrapers. I'd follow him anywhere—even to Hong Kong. We hadn't lived in the same country since we'd met, but this was our chance to be together, to build a life in the city where he grew up.

But one month ago, his company sent him to London.

I first met Ben in London, at a fencing club. I was a bookish American student on a semester abroad. He was an opportunity for a real live English romance, my very own Mr. Darcy, except that unlike Darcy, Ben was talkative—and half Chinese.

I'd taken up fencing several years before, attracted by the romance of sword fighting and the fact that it was something unique, historic, literary even. I wasn't bad, and the sport brought me unexpected confidence. It seemed like a great way for an introvert like me to connect with people at the university in London.

When I pushed open the door to the club, the familiar buzz of the scoring machine and the squeak of athletic shoes on the floor reached my ears. I rocked on the sides of my feet, unsure how to join in. Ben came over immediately, introduced himself, and invited me to fence him. I was relieved at being included and already curious about this open-faced young man whose accent I couldn't place. He won our first bout by one point; he always said I wouldn't have dated him if I had been able to beat him.

We fenced a few more bouts, and then sat cross-legged in our matching gear, masks forgotten on the floor. He prodded at my shy shell; he asked me questions, joked about fencing, told me he was from Hong Kong. He had an eloquent vocabulary mixed with an offbeat sense of humor. He didn't seem to mind when people didn't get his jokes. He put me at ease, and I found myself stealing glances at him as I adjusted my equipment and met the other fencers. By the time I changed my shoes and left the gym, I was already lecturing myself about reading too much into his attention. I didn't want to get swept away, blinded by the novelty of an international fling. But it was too late.

For two months, we wandered the streets of London together, kissed on street corners, and took spontaneous trips to Oxford and the coast. He took the time to get to know me, using our shared love of fencing to get me talking. He surprised me with his insight, his persistence. He seemed to understand why I, analytical and introverted, never quite fit into any group. As someone who had grown up shuttling between Hong Kong and London, not quite Chinese and not quite British, he knew what it was like to be an outsider. Ben had a gift for coaxing people to confide in him and trust him. Before long, he got even the most reserved, responsible American girl to give him handfuls of her heart.

When the semester ended, we said goodbye at Heathrow in a flurry of kisses and long-distance promises: "It will just be for a year, maybe two."

"I can visit you in America."

"I'll get a job wherever you live after graduation," I told him. Our confidence in each other was reckless and optimistic, but staying together felt like the only sensible thing to do.

In 2010, thoroughly in love, I moved to Hong Kong to be with him. It lasted for one glorious month.

Ben left me in Hong Kong on the eve of the Mid-Autumn Festival. Instead of exploring the city with him, I was at the airport saying my goodbyes while the children of Hong Kong flooded the streets and parks with lanterns. Instead of walking beneath the Mid-Autumn moon together, we shared a fierce hug and made a hundred tiny promises. The next day, still reeling from the sheer solitude, I found my way to Tai Hang—to the incense and the drums. The fire dragon loomed, full of possibilities.

It had already grown dark, or as dark as it ever gets in the city, when I emerged from the subway into a night that felt nothing like the end of September. The humidity surrounded me like steam pouring out of a broken dumpling. I made my way along the street. An arch announced the festival in gold foil and tissue paper fringe. I found a spot beside a Chinese family of three or four generations. A group of Mainland girls chattered in shrill Mandarin in front of me. The balconies of a hundred apartments teetered over our heads.

I hadn't had a chance to ask Ben what the fire dragon would be like before the airport security line swallowed him and carried him away. The fire dragon in my mind looked like a dancing, tuft-eared Pekinese dog, with people standing under a big sheet to form the body, holding up the head. Of course, that's an image from a lion dance, not a dragon dance, I would soon learn. I was just starting to discover that Hong Kong was full of surprises—and I was ill prepared. I jumped up on my toes and looked for the Pekinese head.

The drums began. "Want me to hoist you up?" An American man stepped close behind me. He was tall, and the scent of stale beer mixed with the incense.

"No, thanks," I said.

"You sure? You want a good view when they bring out the dragon," he reached for my arms.

"I can see just fine." I maneuvered away from the man, finding refuge on the other side of the Chinese family. My fingers curled tighter around my purse. Suddenly, I was aware just how alone I was in the crowd, and in the country.

"Why didn't you just go to London instead of Hong Kong when you found out Ben would be leaving?" my friends had asked me. "You're already moving across the world for him." I wondered the same thing myself—now. But this was 2010. I wasn't in a position to jet around the world after men lightly. I'd graduated from Colgate University with US$70,000 in student debt, debt I had taken on before the economy crumbled. Moving without a job was not an option. Employment would be hard to find in London for an English major with limited work experience and no visa. I didn't have a chance.

Jobs were not easy to come by anywhere in the Western world. My generation faced the worst job market in living memory. My college-educated friends competed tooth-and-nail for part-time barista work, borrowed more money for graduate school, and moved in with their parents. There was a mounting sense of desperation among those of us who had taken out big student loans only to discover there was no work for us in our own country when we graduated.

Asia was another story.

There were rumors going around that this was where the jobs were to be found. Ben had found work in Hong Kong, his hometown. My own sister had recently begun teaching English in South Korea. So, I spent nearly a year applying and interviewing for a job in Hong Kong (and yes, living with my parents while I did it). When a local school emailed and asked me to be their new English teacher, it seemed the long distance part of our international romance, which had lasted two and a half years by now, was finally done. I showed up with a work visa and a salary advance, ready to take on the city and the next stage in our relationship. Yet here I was, alone in a crowd as the fire dragon approached.

I couldn't afford to give up my new job when Ben's circumstances changed. With a one-way ticket and a monthly student loan payment of US$935, I stayed in Hong Kong.

The drums pounded. A row of children appeared, carrying lanterns that bobbed above the crowds. Their glow mixed with the lights from the apartment buildings looming over our heads. My arms brushed an elbow on one side, a woman's handbag on the other.

Ben had been lucky, really, to be sent to London. It was a one-year placement at a law firm with the prospect of a permanent contract afterwards. All I had to do was spend this year in Hong Kong looking for an opportunity in London where we could be reunited once again. "It'll be for one more year, and then we'll be together," we promised each other as we set up our web-cams. "We already know we can handle the whole long distance thing." We plotted our reunion in a whirl of emails and long distance calls. "It'll just be this year," we said, "and then that's it. No more long distance."

Of course, the other thing people asked was, "What if you don't get along when you finally do live in the same country?" That was a question I couldn't answer.

As I stood in the Mid-Autumn crowd, little did I know that my move to Hong Kong would bring about our longest separation ever, a separation that would bring me face to face with the reality of the risk I had taken.

The pounding of the drums intensified. The people around me drew closer together, choking what little breeze there was. Finally, the fire dragon appeared, followed by more children carrying lanterns. I was surprised when I saw what it was really like. It had an elaborate head, made from branches twisted into intricate shapes and filled with a thicket of incense. The thin body was over 200 feet long and muscular bearers danced beneath its undulating shape. The people around me cheered as the dragon's head passed us and then turned back on itself, leaving behind a million tiny trails of smoke. I felt a growing sense of excitement as the fire dragon whirled and darted through the streets. Its wiry, crackling body defied my expectations. It was fast. It was wild. I pushed forward so I could see better. I was a part of the crowd. I didn't feel like a foreign girl, alone, in an interrupted romance. This was an adventure! I could do this; I could live in Hong Kong, alone. Ben and I would be together soon enough.

As the dragon twirled in front of me, I didn't know that in nine months I'd be sitting on the floor of my single apartment, cell phone pressed to my ear, feeling the foreign ground shift beneath me, feeling a panic I'd been too confident to anticipate. I pulled my hair away from my neck, trying to find relief from the suffocating heat, too stubborn to guess at the coldness that was coming.

This was not what I had planned. Nothing happened the way I expected. This was Hong Kong.

As the rumble of the drums reached a crescendo, the men carrying the dragon pulled off the sticks of incense and passed them to the crowd.

Within seconds, the fire dragon dispersed into a thousand tiny sparks in the night.

2

BEGINNINGS

My jaw was sore from smiling so much. In the first few weeks of work, I stood in the school courtyard wearing a perma-freeze grin and greeting the students as they arrived. Their reactions to me varied: some were puzzled, some were shy, a few laughed, and one little boy had taken to hitting my arms with his tangerine-sized fists to see if I was real.

"Your classes won't start until week three," Helen the English panel chair had told me as she showed me around the school—cafeteria, staff office, English Room. "The class teachers need to teach the routines for the first few weeks. You can greet the students in the morning."

They trailed in through the gates, filling the courtyard with the chatter of first-day jitters. A row of parents pressed their faces against the bars of the fence that surrounded the school. I stood in the midst of the children, and most of their heads didn't reach past my elbows. Two teachers walked by, looking frazzled. They glanced at me, then whispered to each other. I felt like a goldfish getting used to a new bowl of water. A group of little girls stared at me and burst into a fit of giggles. I smiled and waved at them.

Jordan Valley Primary School was in a 'local' area in Kowloon Bay. Dozens of public housing estates surrounded it like a palisade. Most of the young students who lived there had not yet ventured to the parts of Hong Kong that are swarming with Western expatriates. Despite living in a famously international city, my blue-green eyes and light brown hair were unusual to the kids. The youngest ones were not afraid to stare. On my second day, a waist-high girl walked in my direction, fiddling with the bright red string holding her nametag. When she saw me, she jumped, turned as red as her nametag, and darted the other way.

"This is the NET Teacher, Miss Young. Say good morning," Helen told the kids.

"Good morning, Miss Young," they would whisper. They twisted their fingers in light blue uniform dresses and put their hands in the pockets of creased walking shorts.

"How old are you? Say it to Miss Young. How old are you?"

"I am seven years old." They'd look at their feet, then at Helen, and then glance up at me through fine black eyelashes before quickly looking back at their shoes.

The children parted around me like ducklings when I walked through the courtyard. Helen coaxed more greetings out of them, more rote responses. She had a mother's smile, a Sunday School teacher's voice. "Lily, say good morning to Miss Young."

One brave boy came up to speak to me by himself on the third day. He was carrying a clipboard and his shorts were hiked up high on his waist.

"Good morning, Miss Young!" he said.

"Good morning." I smiled as he looked at me through glasses perched on the bridge of his nose.

"My name is Anthony. I am an English Ambassador. My English is very good." Each word was clipped and carefully separated.

"Hello Anthony. Your English is very good indeed," I said, matching his formal tone.

"I would like to practice my English with you. It is nice to meet you."

"That's a good idea. It's nice to meet you, too." Anthony smiled at me and wandered off. He spoke to me regularly after that, eager for the chance to practice his English. I was glad to have a friend.

Each morning before the bell rang the students assembled in perfect lines. They bowed to the principal, the teachers, and each other, and listened quietly to the morning announcements. Over 500 six-to-twelve-year-olds stood as still as terra-cotta statues. After the announcements finished, the teachers led their classes toward the stairs. As the kids filed past me, still in their perfect lines, I continued to wave and smile determinedly. By my fourth day the children's double takes were being replaced with tentative waves and shy smiles.

When the last line of bobbing heads and heavy backpacks reached the steps, I rode the elevator up to the teachers' office on the fifth floor. Every once in a while the local teachers would pop into the office, but no one spoke to me, and only a few smiled. They stammered and blushed when I said hello.

I was the only foreigner at the school. My official title was the NET Teacher (Native English-speaking Teacher). The Hong Kong Education Bureau paid for one native English-speaking teacher in every public school in the region. It was largely up to the schools to decide how they wanted to make use of their NET. In my case, they didn't give me very much work to do, especially at the start. It was my job to stand and deliver my American smile and my American "good morning".

The last NET teacher at this school, an older British man, had stayed for only two months. I still hadn't learned the full story, but I gathered he could not adjust to the new environment. No one would give me a straight answer about why he left so quickly. Was the school that bad? All I knew was that the teachers and students had gotten used to not having a NET.

As the local teachers began their classes, there were weeks before I'd need to teach. I felt detached. This was an exciting opportunity to experience a new culture; it was also a job and I wanted to do it well. Yet nearly every word that made its way to my ears was incomprehensible, every laugh from across the room, a mystery. I was an oddity and an aberration, listening to the Cantonese clamor around me.

"Is there anything I should be doing to prepare?" I had asked Helen on the phone before I left the US. "Do you have a book list that I should read ahead of time, or maybe a textbook I should look at?"

"No, no. Just take a rest during the summer. No need to prepare."

"So, I'll have time to write lesson plans when I get there?"

"Oh yes, no need to worry," she had said.

As I rearranged files on my computer and flipped through a stack of picture books, I thought about the paper trail that brought me there. As a textbook overachiever in high school, I studied hard, got involved in extracurricular activities, and held all the right leadership positions to do what I wanted with my life (my plan: go to a liberal arts college that had pretty, tree-lined drives and become a book editor). My parents were supportive, but they didn't have to push me because I was pushing myself. I was my very own tiger mother.

When I got into my ideal college on the East Coast, Colgate University in New York, I continued my pattern of hard work and overachievement. My semester in London was the only time I didn't also have a job while taking a full load of classes (I kept busy gallivanting around with Ben). After college, while I was trying to figure out a way to get back to him while still making my student loan payments, I spent a year teaching at a charter school in my hometown and devoted every waking hour to grading papers and writing student evaluations. As I plotted my move to Hong Kong, I read about the city and what to expect, haunting expat forums and grilling Ben about Chinese work culture. Hong Kong was fast-paced, even frantic. Diligence was in the air and the water. Surely, I should fit right in.

Instead, I was adrift in a job with low expectations, facing an unconventional kind of culture shock. I hadn't had this much time on my hands since 8th grade. I wasn't sure what to do.

I walked over to check on the spacious English Room, which had been decorated before my arrival. When I passed the windows of the other classrooms, the students lifted their heads from their textbooks and watched me, whispering to each other until their teachers shouted at them.

Our school building was new, but as I stood outside my classroom I was puzzled to see a big construction site next door to us that was slowly morphing into another primary school. Helen sat her desk when I returned to the staffroom. She was far more comfortable speaking to me than the rest of the teachers. I peeked over the top of the cubicle wall. "Why are they building a new school right next door?" I asked.

"This area is growing. There is lots of new housing being built here."

"Will we be collaborating with that school?" I imagined a NET teacher best friend next door, already picturing us walking home together after school.

"No. We will be competitors. We want to attract the good students in this area." She looked somewhat apologetic.

"Oh..." I decided to change the subject. "Do people usually have big families in Hong Kong?"

"I have four sisters," she told me. "One lives in USA and one lives in UK. The others live in Hong Kong."

Unlike Mainland China, Hong Kong has never had a one-child policy, but I was surprised. "Is that common?" I asked. I came from a big family myself (two boys and seven girls) and I was used to being an anomaly. I thought we had a big family back when there were just four of us.

"Not so many any more because it is very expensive."

"Why do they need so much new housing then?"

"Many people are coming over from Mainland China. Many of our students' parents come from there," she said. "It is cheap government housing here." She gestured to the row of identical apartment blocks standing guard outside the window.

This was the first I heard about a trend that was changing Hong Kong almost beyond recognition. After 156 years as a British colony, Hong Kong belonged to China again. Since the Handover in 1997, many members of the vast population of China had decided that this was where they wanted to pursue a better life. They were pouring into Hong Kong to take up jobs, both professional and menial, and to spend their newly acquired wealth. Those who were not already part of the mushrooming nouveau riche worked themselves to the bone to find their fortune in Hong Kong.

"So do the parents at our school speak English? Do they teach English in China like they do here?" I asked Helen.

"Only about twenty percent learned English in secondary school, and most of them do not feel comfortable with speaking," she said. "Less than half of the parents were born in Hong Kong." This explained why I wouldn't have to participate in parent-teacher conferences. Helen told me that since many of our students were the children of Mainland Chinese, they faced the usual adaptive challenges of immigrant children, even though Hong Kong was once again part of China and still 95% Chinese. It was an uphill battle to learn English and sometimes also Cantonese, the dialect of Chinese spoken in Hong Kong. I could relate. However, these kids had a chance that their parents did not have. Hong Kong for them was a place to reinvent yourself. Unlike in the struggling United States, anything seemed possible.

I was there for the opportunities too, but I struggled to find my place, feeling guilty that I wasn't doing more. The teachers rushed to their classes around me, already busy with marking and prep. It felt odd doing so little in this vibrant, frantic city. I was out of step, not at all sure that I'd made the right decision to stay, even though it seemed like my only option. Perhaps I should have gone home to America…

As the days passed at the school, the kids still stared and I towered awkwardly over my co-workers in the elevator. I tried striking up a conversation with another teacher who was also new, Mr. Liu. He was an attractive, clean-cut young man, the only teacher who was as tall as me. "Is this your first year teaching?"

"No. I have been a teacher for ten years," he said shortly. He hadn't spoken to me since.

In the sultry heat of the afternoons, I'd trudge along the pavement beneath 30-floor apartment blocks, looking for lunch, thinking about Ben. I tried to picture him swearing he'd never leave me alone again, no matter what it did to his career prospects. But no. He was on the other side of the world, getting used to a new job of his own.

One afternoon, an old Chinese man broke my self-pitying reverie. As I walked past, he said, "Hello, where are you from?"

"The US," I replied, surprised at being addressed.

"Ah yes. Which state in the US?" He was taller than me, and he wore a nicely pressed white shirt and a safari hat. He seemed bemused to encounter a white lady here beneath the projects.

"Arizona."

"Ah yes, my daughter lives in Seattle, and it's not often that I get to talk with people in English. Are you in Hong Kong for a job?"

I didn't generally make a habit of telling strange men on the street all about myself, but I instinctively trusted this grandfatherly gentleman. Besides, I needed someone to talk to. Squinting into his kind face, I told my new Chinese friend a little bit about myself. He was a retired physics teacher who had also been the principal of a secondary school for many years. We chatted as toddlers skipped past in minuscule preschool uniforms and old women fanned themselves and watched us from the nearby benches. He thanked me for the conversation. "Next time I will speak to you in Chinese," he said.

I went on my way, thinking about the old man's words. It reminded me of another time a stranger had spoken to me in a foreign city. My first move abroad had set in motion the runaway train of events that brought me to Hong Kong, and to Ben.

In the fall of my junior year of college, I moved to London to study for a semester. Mostly due to an obsession with British literature, I'd always felt drawn to England, but this was the first time I had been there. As I was dragging my overstuffed suitcase, laptop, and fencing equipment bag down the street from the train station, a woman in a rumpled sweater called out, "You ought to get yourself a bloke to help you carry those!" Her words turned out to be prophetic.

I lived with four friends in a beautiful old flat in Bloomsbury, right around the corner from where Charles Dickens, Edgar Allan Poe and Virginia Woolf used to live. I loved everything about the city. As a long time anglophile, it was a romance that was bound to happen. London was dynamic and relevant, but you could see 2,000 years' worth of history just by walking down the street. I loved the little blue signs that indicated where famous literary and historical people used to dwell, the accents and languages pouring from people on the streets, the bridges showing a dozen different panoramas on the Thames. I was on a serious high already, and then I walked into that fencing club and met a Eurasian law student with a strong jaw, stand-on-end black hair, and subtle freckles.

Ben and I took it slow and enjoyed each other's company before we started dating. He took the time to get through my reserved exterior. In fact, I don't think we talked about anything except fencing for the first month. He told me later he wasn't sure he'd be able to break past my shell and figure out what I was really like. I already desperately hoped that he liked me, but I was determined not to make too much of his friendliness. I tried to play it cool. He took me to some eclectic bars and a friend's house party, not realizing I was as uninterested in partying as he was. He convinced me to go to Switzerland with the fencing team and contrived to sit next to me on the plane. Finally, one chilly London night, he decided to be direct.

Earlier in the evening we'd had dinner in Chinatown. We'd been seated at a large round table with a group of Chinese women. Ben told me later he could understand every word of their Cantonese, and it had been difficult to talk comfortably. I'd retreated inward, getting quieter than normal, and Ben grew frustrated. He tried to interrupt the tension by suggesting we go on an adventure to find the Freemasons' headquarters. Then he took me to a chic bar whose interior had been designed by a friend of his, a woman who also came from Hong Kong. We sat on low couches with our knees not quite touching. It was crowded and noisy. The conversation waned, and I worried that we had finally exhausted our usual topic: fencing. Maybe our relationship, whatever it was, had run its course. A silence stretched between us, battered by the chatter and the music. Finally, he leaned forward and looked into my eyes. "I feel like this could go one of two ways," he said. "We've had a nice time hanging out, but I can't tell if you want any more than that. I don't really like dating games where no one can just be honest about how they feel."

"I don't want to play games either." I couldn't look away from his face.

"If you don't like me, we can just say we've had a good time so far and leave it at that." There was a clarity and an intensity in his hazel eyes that made me uncomfortable, but I felt like I could step into that discomfort and be completely myself.

"I do like you. I've been having a good time."

"Do you want to get to know me," he said, "and just be honest about how things are going—if they keep going?"

I did.

He took my hands and ran his fingers along the inside of my wrists, creating a riot in my stomach that matched the throb of the music. We put our heads together and talked for hours—the awkwardness shattered.

I don't remember what we said, but it was like we'd broken through a barrier, a shield of politeness and reserve that I'd developed as a shy child. It was a barrier that usually took years for friends to get through, but Ben was on the other side of it already, and it felt completely natural.

Ben had moved to England for boarding school when he was thirteen. With his mixed-race face and international outlook, he was out of place among the English, even after living there for ten years, but he did not quite fit in with the Chinese either. Like many Hong Kong-raised Brits, Ben had always felt a sense of unbelonging. Hong Kong was transient, especially for international families like his. If you were from there it was easy to feel like you came from nowhere. This was particularly true of the child of one expatriate Brit and one local Chinese woman. Ben knew what it was like to be an outsider. When I arrived on the scene, an American abroad who had always felt out of place in the USA, we clicked.

Perhaps I was naïve, and treated it as part of the study abroad experience, but it was exciting to compare our different cultures as we got to know each other. Some of the differences were unexpected. We bought cooking ingredients one evening and lugged them back to his place in a black London cab. I thought it would be a time to flirt and have fun, but Ben approached the food with shocking concentration, his thick eyebrows pulled low. Every combination had to be perfect, every dish had to be tested multiple times. It was the only time he was quiet and I was the one saying, "Don't be so serious!" He blew out a long, heavy breath when I said, "It's just food!" It was my first indication of the importance of food to a Hong Kong person. The rest of the time, Ben led the banter. He could talk to anyone about anything, meeting them where they were most comfortable, inviting their confidences, winning their admiration—and mine.

What girl wouldn't be swept away by a fairytale English romance? He took me ice-skating in a refurbished palace on a hilltop and fencing at a private club in an 18th-century building. I took him swing dancing in a famous old jazz bar and told him about my aspirations, my bookish passions. We bought a pizza and climbed over the locked gates of Regent's Park to eat it in the moonlight. (It sounds romantic, but actually, when Ben climbed back over the gate he ripped an eight-inch gash in the crotch of his jeans. He could barely hold the flaps of denim together and I could barely hold in my laughter as we made our way back to his place.) We watched the stars from Primrose Hill. We took the train south and hiked for miles along the English coast, exploring the bluffs and the downs and the lonely lighthouses. Looking back, those first months sound like the montage section of a chick flick, complete with scenes of us kissing under an umbrella on a rainy street corner.

The only catch to the whole lovely affair was, of course, that I was going back to America.

I returned to the school, walking past an old woman burning paper on the sidewalk. Bits of ash drifted over the street, swirling in the wake of the passing taxis.

3

A ROOM WITH A VIEW

The sleek, ultra-efficient MTR train deposited me in a different world, a world where fire dragons were quaint and luxury was god: Central, my new home. I walked through the crowds in the station and ascended into the fancy office building/shopping mall above it. The polished floors reflected the lights from Dior and Bottega Veneta. At any hour, well-heeled shoppers mingled with the suits walking back and forth between the office towers. Covered walkways spanned the gaps between the skyscrapers. You didn't even have to touch the ground when you walked from one side of Central to the other. It was nothing like the China I'd heard stories of growing up, a land of crowded trains, exotic foods, and boats with painted eyes floating on the yellow waters of the Yangtze River. Hong Kong radiated wealth, ambition, and modernity.

Central was an office worker's paradise; everything you could possibly need, every convenience, every resource, every commercial coffee shop, was right at your fingertips. It was a place in which to be lost, anonymous.

It took just seven minutes to walk to my apartment from the Central MTR station. I'd find my way beneath the skyscrapers and climb past the Coach store, one-of-a-kind boutiques, an iconic tourist lane, and hidden restaurants. My building sat at the edge of SoHo, home to bars and restaurants with food from every part of the world frequented by expatriates from every part of the world. There was a healthy smoothie bar on the ground floor and a shady nightclub called the Buddha Lounge in the basement. When I left for work in the mornings, there were often still a few partiers in black leather guzzling beer on the steps outside the Buddha, the music pumping dully in the early morning sun.

My street was called Hollywood Road. Named after a country estate in Ireland, not the Hollywood in California, it was a nod to the inexorable Western influence in Hong Kong. It was famous for antique shops and modern art galleries. At one end, the shops held Hindu goddess statues, carved ivory tusks, and jade in countless shapes and sizes. And of course, there were dragons. At the other end, the modern art galleries displayed statues of pigs getting suction cup massages, beautiful paintings of young girls dressed in soldiers' uniforms, and abstract impressionist works in every dissonant and harmonic color combination imaginable. In the middle of the street, right around my building, the two types of shops, old and new, mixed.

Slicing through Hollywood Road, right beside my building, was the Mid-levels Escalator, the longest outdoor covered escalator in the world. It carried people back and forth between the offices and shops of Central and the apartments and luxury condos that filled the middle of Victoria Peak. Since its completion in 2003, the Escalator had birthed a new corridor of life on the way up the hill. Every hundred yards or so, you could climb down and find restaurants and shops, galleries and bars. As you rode up the hill, the windows on either side advertised Cuban cigars, nail salons, designers, and set dinners.

Just a few steps away from my door, I could enter Sheung Wan, a district that was all about local flavor. This was where I found the Hong Kong I had imagined as I prepared to join Ben in Asia. There were market stalls selling fruit, flowers, and vegetables, and butcher shops with pigs' heads and whole ducks hanging in the windows. I once saw one quarter of some sort of ram or goat hanging in a shop. It had been sliced so its head, one horn, one hoof, one shoulder, and one leg were all still attached. There were fish hawkers, too. Theoretically, I could pick a live fish or crab out of a tank on the street and take it home to cook for dinner. The smell of the market was pungent: the sickly odor of raw meat that has been sitting in the fresh air all day mixed with whiffs of vehicle exhaust and the earthy smell of root vegetables. The vegetables were laid out on tables like crayons; deep purple roots, hot pink dragonfruit, leafy green cabbages and heavy, multi-colored squash. I didn't recognize some of the produce that languished in the sun, wilting under the scrutiny of the shoppers.

The first day I bought vegetables from one of the food stands, I nearly died. I handed a few coins to the smiling man at the stall and took a step back. Suddenly, he grabbed my arm and pulled me forward. A white van shot through the narrow street behind me. It took a few seconds to figure out what had happened, but the man just chuckled. The busy market was not restricted to pedestrians. The cars mixed right in with the old women carrying grocery bags and the photographers taking pictures of a famous local restaurant. Each day, I mixed with them too as I found my way through Central's labyrinth.

With no one waiting for me at home, after work I'd often stop to visit one of the bastions of Western culture in the East: Starbucks. A grande iced coffee at Starbucks in Hong Kong costs about six bucks—more than a bowl of noodles—but the place was humming with a comforting, Westernized bustle. I'd watch the bankers, lawyers, and tourists settling into comfy chairs surrounded by the familiar smell of French roast.

All around me, the professionals, international and local, would roll up their sleeves, pull out their computers, and get down to networking and, I imagined, some serious creative brainstorming. I wanted to be part of it. Before I met Ben—and the economy fell to bits—I had planned to work in publishing in New York City. I imagined drinking coffee with authors and lunching with agents between bouts of feverish red-pen work. I'd dreamed of Manhattan, and then of London, when I met Ben. As I watched the people in Central, wrapped up in money and ideas, those images came back to me in a rush of displacement. Hong Kong was far away from the life I had planned.

In those early days, I'd linger for as long as I could justify taking up a chair, and I'd read. Books were my substitute friends in a lonely environment. The first thing I read in Hong Kong was Forster's *A Room With a View*. It's about a young woman going abroad for the first time, discovering passion and art and independence. Like me, Ms. Honeychurch finds herself wrapped up in a love story enhanced by an exotic city, like my London days, like the romance I had hoped for in Hong Kong. But I was alone. I'd picked the book because I had just moved into a little room with a view.

My apartment amidst the shabby little fruit stands, futuristic high-rises, art galleries and restaurants boasted one of the best views in Hong Kong. From my window on the 13th floor, I could look directly into the courtyard of the old Central Police Station complex. The main building featured big stone columns and a slate gray façade jutting into the sky. It was so straight that it appeared to hang over the pedestrians looking up. The big front doors were barred and padlocked and looked like they hadn't been opened in fifty years. Behind it, three floors of staff barracks surrounded the concrete expanse of the courtyard. Whitewashed open-air colonnades ran the length of the barracks buildings. It looked like something straight out of an old British Army film.

Behind the barracks building, I could see the rusty bars and solemn red brick of the old Victoria Prison. The structure had been unused for years, and it looked dense and solitary against the glittering teeth of the Mid-levels high-rises. The whole compound had been standing empty since the police headquarters moved over to a bigger and more modern complex in Wan Chai. That's where most of the crime went too.

When I first read the advertisement for the apartment, I thought it would be depressing to live above a gloomy old prison building. But the view changed my mind. There was something incredibly romantic about being able to see one of the last remaining relics of colonial Britain in Hong Kong from my window. As I gazed down on the imposing structure sitting locked and empty in a city that was literally bursting at the seams with people, I felt like it belonged to me. It was something to hold onto when Ben flew away.

My partially furnished apartment was bright and cozy. It had a narrow bedroom and a narrow living room, with a tiny square kitchen through one door and a bathroom with a green marble shower through another. Ben had helped me find it. We went to an estate agent together one Saturday afternoon right before he left for London. He cracked jokes in Cantonese with the women in the tiny ground floor office as they talked about the area. He insisted on a safe building with a doorman, and I asked for a washing machine. They introduced us to their associate, Edmund, who took us to see the place on Hollywood Road.

"Yes, many people want such a view," lisped Edmund, his long, thin hands twisting around the spare keys. "You are getting a good deal for a view like this. And such a good location too!"

Ben and I tried out the black pleather couch, looking out the window as the sun's rays splintered off the glass of the high-rises and lingered on the old stone columns. "Do you think I'm really getting a good deal?" I whispered. The rent was more than I would spend in student loan payments each month. It was probably more than it would cost to rent my parents' seven-bedroom house in Arizona.

"I'm sure he says that to customers all the time, but yeah, this is a great location," he said.

"Should I look closer to my school, just in case?"

"You don't want to live that far out. Trust me, it'll be a lot easier for you to stay on Hong Kong Island."

"It might be cheaper." I could almost buy two plane tickets to London for the cost of the rent—and the apartment was less than 300 square feet!

"Hong Kong is all about the convenience. It'll be easier to find whatever you need around here. And you'll be closer to my place."

"The least you can do is stay with me when you visit," I mumbled. Ben had been living with his parents while he worked in the city.

"My mum will want to see me too. Anyway, this is a short walk from everything. You'll love it. Trust me." I would come to appreciate the convenience of the location later, but I was already enamored of the view.

Although Ben had helped me move into my apartment and showed me where to buy essentials, I did not yet feel settled. Hong Kong was frantic, electric. I stood out uncomfortably in some areas, got lost in others. I was confused about how to feel. Should I be excited to be living in such a glamorous and varied place? Distressed that I had moved to Asia for a man who had just moved to Europe? I was confident that things would work out with Ben, but was that the right feeling? Had I made the right choice? *Would* we be together next year?

I thought back to when we had made the original decision to try a long distance relationship. Our romance had been worthy of a storybook, but that didn't change the fact that I had to go back to the US to finish my degree—and we had known each other for barely three months.

One winter evening, we went to a party at the home of Ben's old friend Selena. Ben and Selena had known each other since primary school in Hong Kong. Both of them had ended up in London. I was anxious to get the stamp of approval from one of his friends. It was a poker party, and I managed to make a good impression by winning the first round, though I lost everything after that. Before long, Ben and I moved away from the poker table and ended up talking in the kitchen with Selena's sister, Evie. She leaned back against the kitchen counter, tapping her glittering stilettos against the linoleum, and asked me, "So, when are you going back to America?"

"In two weeks."

"Well, what are you going to do then? Just break up?"

Her question made me look deep into my soda. "We haven't really talked about it yet."

"You like each other, right?"

"Yes, we really do," Ben put in.

"Well, it's not like long distance relationships work. Can you stay in London?"

"I have to finish college."

"So you'll break up."

"I'm not sure." No one had asked the question before and we'd been avoiding it. We didn't want to jinx the early days of our romance by talking about our future.

That evening we took the night bus back into central London. We sat in the first row of seats on the upper deck of the bus and watched the city lights go by. "So, Evie was nice," I began. Ben was quiet for a moment.

"You know, she doesn't always think before she speaks."

"That's okay. I don't think she was being mean." The bus swung around Trafalgar Square, Nelson standing austere on his column beside us.

"She's always been like that. It's an interesting question though. What do you think?"

"Yup, interesting." I waited.

"So—" we both spoke at the same time.

"You go first," I said.

"Would you like to be my girlfriend?"

I felt my stomach do a little leap, and it wasn't just because the bus flew around a curve like Stan Shunpike was driving. "For the next two weeks?" I asked.

"Or for longer."

"Yes, I would like that," I paused, then pressed on. "You know, I'm really interested in living in London eventually, and I might be able to get an internship here in the summertime. We can see how things go."

"Yes, let's see how things go. The truth is I don't want to say goodbye in two weeks." I leaned on his shoulder, our fingers intertwined, and the bus lumbered through the nighttime traffic. Fourteen days later, Ben helped me carry my suitcases back to the airport and I left him behind. Tears caught like cement in the back of my throat.

From then on, Ben and I saw each other roughly every three months, sometimes for a week, sometimes for a month, in one country or another. Then the economic downturn prevented me from moving to London after college and sent Ben to Hong Kong. I remember the way my stomach squeezed tight as graduation approached. The news preached doom and economic gloom, and I realized we wouldn't be together immediately. My student loans weighed on my mind as I accepted a job in Arizona and moved home. Then, Ben got a singular opportunity at a London firm just as I was finalizing my move to Asia.

We had talked on the phone, emailed, instant messaged, or talked on webcam nearly every day for two and a half years. Skype had become our best friend. Ten years ago, it wouldn't have been possible for us to communicate the way we did now. The time was right for an international long distance relationship. Even so, we had to live in the same city some day. We had to make sure we were really right for each other. I had to know if Ben's offbeat jokes would wear on me over time, or if they would continue to be endearing. Would our cultural differences continue to excite and challenge us, or would I wake up beside him in a foreign country one day and wish for home? Every time we saw each other, the rush of wonder and affection would obliterate our worries. We gloried in our adventures, living in a perpetual vacation. It would be the same when we saw each other regularly—right?

Outside my window, the Central Police Station complex was an island of calm, unchanged. I thought about the British officials and the Chinese policemen who had lived and worked behind those walls. What did Hong Kong look like to them? What choices did they face? I wondered if anyone hid there when the Japanese occupied Hong Kong during World War II. I wondered how many men lived out the rest of their days behind those prison bars. What was going to happen to those lonely old buildings as Hong Kong rushed headlong into the future?

I hung pictures in my apartment, surrounded by constant reminders of Hong Kong's past, present and future, wondering what my own future would hold.

4

LUNCH ADVENTURES

I had taken all of my breaks at work alone so far. Helen usually brought a boxed lunch to school so she could keep working, and I was too shy to invite myself along with the other teachers. I'd slowly been getting to know the neighborhood around the school by myself. But one day, I turned out of the school gates and a little lady with round glasses jumped out of an alleyway and shouted into my ear, "You like Japanese noodle?!" When my heart stopped having a boxing match with my ribs, I nodded yes. Beyond her, the alleyway was filled with members of the school's teaching staff, all about to head to their favorite Japanese noodle joint. "We will take the taxi!" my new friend said. The other teachers nodded encouragingly. They hustled me into a taxi and we were off.

The driver catapulted his vehicle around every turn and didn't pay attention to which lane he was in or whether the lanes around him were occupied. I gripped the teacher next to me, catching glimpses of the surrounding neighborhood. Massive apartment blocks flashed by. The teachers chattered loudly in Cantonese. The language was sometimes guttural, sometimes shrill. I was too distracted by the careening of the vehicle to try to guess what they were saying.

At the restaurant we found more teachers saving our seats and carrying on a lively, shouted conversation with the chef behind the counter. The place was small and almost all the tables were full. A group of men in the black-pants-and-white-shirt uniform of salesmen were sharing plates of sashimi. Two teenage girls were taking pictures of their food with their iPhones. A young Filipina helped a wrinkled old woman stand up from her chair. I was ushered to a seat by a rotund lady who taught English and Mandarin. She asked if I needed an English menu. "No thanks, I'll just point to the words and hope for the best." She laughed and patted me on the back.

Cantonese conversation washed over me as I ordered what luckily turned out to be a bowl of noodles with pork. Sometimes they'd ask me a question or drop in an English phrase like, "So busy!" I learned that one of the men lived on Hong Kong Island, like me, but most of the others lived somewhere in Kowloon. I listened to the tone and tempo of the conversation without understanding its meaning.

Our food arrived, and I picked up my chopsticks. The entire group turned to look at me. I pinched a mouthful of slippery noodles. When I realized they were watching me eat, I went for a piece of pork at the same time. I lifted the bite to my mouth without a single drip.

"Ooooh! Very good! You can use the chopsticks!" They congratulated me in unison. My dad had taught me to use chopsticks when I was a child. He had his own ties to Asia. But more on that later...

"So, what are your English names?" I asked. Everyone had an English first name in Hong Kong.

"I am Flora, and she is also Flora," said Flora, the bespectacled woman who had invited me to lunch.

"I can remember that."

"And she is... Miss Lo what is your English name?" Flora asked.

"I am Olivia," said the rotund language teacher.

"Okay, Olivia, and Miss Pong is Rita." I would quickly discover that the teachers rarely used their English names. They did not interact with foreigners very often. Most of them didn't know each other's English names at all. I called them all Miss Poon or Mister Chan or Miss Ng, just like the kids did.

After lunch we all went for ice cream at a local favorite, McDonald's, and then strolled back to the school. We passed shops, eateries and housing agents along the way. Flora pointed to an appliance store, with washers and toasters clearly visible in the window, and told me I could get washers and toasters there, and then she pointed to a fruits and vegetables stand and told me I could get fruits and vegetables there. She even held my arm to make sure I crossed the street safely. I appreciated her efforts.

"Do you know the shop OK?" Flora asked.

"Okay?"

She pointed to a familiar sign. "It is for snacks and drinks."

"Oh, you mean Circle K?"

"You have this shop in USA?"

"Yes, I think it's actually an American brand."

"Aiyaa, I didn't know you have this shop in USA."

The next day, Flora invited me to join them for lunch again, and we took another harrowing taxi ride to the Japanese noodle place. We were regular customers. The chef gave us free appetizers, like dishes of shrimp in a spicy oil that tasted vaguely of oysters. Sometimes we got lucky and were presented with little bowls of tiny octopuses in a rich, honey-sweet sauce. They tasted great as long as you didn't think about the suction cups grabbing at you as they slid down your throat.

I soon learned why we went to this particular Japanese restaurant, apart from the free seafood. Long before we finished eating, my cheery, bespectacled friend began waving for the check. As soon as it arrived, one of the PE teachers, a young-at-heart type who wore a shell on a cord around his neck, bolted out of the restaurant and down the street. I noticed a mounting sense of excitement around the table, and people started talking about "one hundred dollar!" and nodding reassuringly at me.

As we slurped up the last of our noodles, the PE teacher returned with two 50 HKD gift certificates for the Wellcome grocery store clutched triumphantly in his hand. The whole table cheered. We quickly gathered our things and headed out the door. I learned that the shopping center nearby offered grocery store vouchers to people who brought in bills from the local restaurants paired with taxi receipts.

We proceeded merrily down to the store and split the $100 between the seven of us. 100 HKD is about fifteen bucks, so the gift certificates allowed each of us to buy about 2 USD worth of sweets.

"What did you buy? What did you buy?" they asked each other. Most people held up a piece of candy or two. Olivia was content with a jar of jam. Mr. Choy, who had a peaceful, almost zen-like face, held up a four-pack of Minute Maid orange juice that he had found for just a few dollars.

"Oh! Very good! Very clever!" Flora number two exclaimed.

I showed off my large bag of M&Ms.

By the time we got back to school I had learned two new Cantonese phrases: "it's too hot" and "so happy!" Flora, of the enthusiasm and the spectacles, told me, "We play again tomorrow!"

During the next two lunches, we managed to convince the restaurant to give us an extra meal receipt to redeem for the gift certificates. A different teacher went to collect the vouchers each time so that whoever was giving them out in exchange for receipts from local restaurants wouldn't realize it was always us. "Miss Young should take the receipt," Miss Pong said, and the whole group dissolved into laughter.

On one afternoon, the diminutive teacher who took the receipts returned with a bottle of cheap white wine in addition to the gift certificates. She'd won the daily sweepstakes prize. We gathered sheepishly around the bottle in the shopping mall, hoping that none of the parents from our school would walk by. I wish I could say we took our prize back to the faculty lounge and shared it in a cross-cultural, totally-against-school-policy bonding session, but we didn't. I don't know who took the wine home.

On Friday, we snagged an extra receipt again, guaranteeing us a full 200 HKD (30 USD) to split among us. It was a fitting end to our week of lunches out as we collected cookies, snacks, and drinks to stock our desks. After the third week of school we could no longer take long lunch breaks. Now all my lunches would be steamed vegetables, meat and rice from the school cafeteria. The half days were over and the real work of the school year was about to begin.

As we strolled out of the Wellcome, Mr. Choy with the peaceful face suddenly pulled out another 50 HKD gift certificate. I have no idea where this one came from, but we all cheered anyway and went back to the store. Flora told me we would play again during exam week in January.

5

EXPLORING MONG KOK

Despite my lunchtime camaraderie with my co-workers, I worried I wouldn't make any friends my own age in Hong Kong. Some expats arrive and immediately begin a frantic tour of the city's social scene, led by boozy co-workers and bookended by happy hour and brunch. Friendship is fast, cheap, and interchangeable in the expat world. But as the only foreigner at my school, I was missing that crucial first link. After-hours social engagements were not forthcoming at the school either. The teachers constantly talked about how busy they were. They didn't have the energy in the middle of their hectic days to speak English to me, and none of them socialized after work, even with each other. Besides, I was still an interesting guest on the other side of a cultural divide.

I spent my evenings and weekends alone, at first. The time difference meant that Ben was always leaving for work as I was getting home. It was getting harder to arrange mid-week dinner/breakfast dates over webcam, leaving me with even more time in solitude. I watched more TV in those first months than in the previous five years combined. Sometimes I cooked pasta and watched the lights come on in the high-rises that climbed the brow of Victoria Peak. But there was only so much time I could spend watching the abandoned building beneath my window and writing emails to my far-away lover. Biting loneliness was nibbling at my ankles.

In vulnerable moments, when the solitude stopped being romantic and just became sad, I'd think, "Enough is enough. I'm going to quit my job and jump on the first plane to London." I wanted to share my whole life with Ben, not just ten-minute phone calls every few days and the occasional weekend Skype chat. I was not the only person ever to feel the every-day drain of a long distance relationship, but I had already been patient for two and a half years. A part of me wondered how much longer I would last.

Finally, I ventured out into Hong Kong one Saturday, determined to get acquainted with my adopted city. It was time to combat the loneliness by throwing myself into a crowded new world.

Hong Kong consists of several islands of various sizes and a chunk of land separated from Mainland China by a border crossing. Hong Kong Island is the financial center and the most famous of the islands that make up the Special Administrative Region. The south side of the island is mainly residential. Luxurious high rises climb up the hills surrounding the bays and coves of the South China Sea. The north side of the island is a densely packed metropolis full of futuristic walkways and the highest concentration of skyscrapers in the world. The city stretches the length of the island, and it seems like every spare inch is at least ten stories tall. My building was right in the middle of all this activity.

Directly across a stretch of water called Victoria Harbour lies Kowloon. If Central is Hong Kong's Manhattan, Kowloon is Brooklyn, another densely packed city full of people and shops and noise. On this particular weekend, I tackled one of the more colorful areas of Kowloon: Mong Kok. I took the MTR beneath the harbor. From the moment the train doors opened, people surrounded me. I held my elbows close to my sides and looked above the short, dark heads that crowded my field of vision. The little dots on the MTR map lit up as we passed each station, making the jump underneath the harbor in a few short minutes. Three stops later, I joined the rush out of the doors and up the escalators and exited into the Saturday madness that is Mong Kok.

The press of people overwhelmed me as I emerged into the sunlight. Everyone seemed to know where they were going, but weren't in a hurry to get there. Little families, young couples, chattering older women, aggressive workers and dazed tourists surrounded me as I looked for landmarks or hints that I was going in the right direction. Everywhere I turned, ads and signs shouted about the goods and services to be found in every available space on the street. The buildings towered ten and twenty stories above me and were filled to the brim with shops and people. Advertisements hung out of some windows and laundry on lines waved down at me from others.

People carrying shopping bags filled the streets. Hong Kong is famous for its shopping, and Mong Kok was one of the best places to get affordable goods of any kind. I was on a mission to find a portable external hard drive for the thousands and thousands of pictures I had taken in my travels as one half of an international relationship. I pulled myself together and started pushing through the crowds. There was a computer mall somewhere in Mong Kok, so that was what I had to find.

At one street corner I made a lucky guess and turned in the direction of the computer mall. I climbed the stairs into the packed interior of the building. Narrow aisles separated little shops selling every type of electronic item under the sun. The aisles were full of people, the air heavy with the smell of sweat, plastic, and the dampness of a leaking air-conditioning unit. Every time someone stopped to examine a gadget, a mini traffic jam would ensue, everyone pushing any way they could in the cramped space.

Like most Americans, I liked to maintain a bubble of personal space, but here any hope of comfort had to be abandoned at the door. I should have left my personal space bubble in Arizona where it belonged. At any given moment I was touching at least six people. Nevertheless, I tackled the crowds and found a stall with the portable hard drives.

Wires, drives, sockets and cases dripped from the thin walls of the shop and miscellaneous electronic accessories hung from the low ceiling like overripe fruit. The walls were punctuated by LCD screens flashing the music videos of Korean pop groups and Lady Gaga. I couldn't hear the music over the multilingual banter between the slim, college-age guys selling the products and the mass of shoppers. By the time I'd paid for my drive and forced my way back through the aisles, I was feeling claustrophobic, but proud of myself. This was a real, local thing to do! I could have found an external hard drive at a sleek Westernized shopping mall, but I decided I definitely paid less in Mong Kok.

It was time for a drink and a snack. For a brief second I caught myself looking for a Starbucks, but then I determinedly marched up to one of the food stands on the side of the road. There was a whole array of street food in Hong Kong, and not all of it was particularly appetizing. I looked at the steaming trays of squishy, round balls that looked like a cross between a meatball and a donut hole and pointed them out to the woman behind the counter. She spooned a few of them out of an oily, curry-colored sauce and plopped them into a brown paper bag with a toothpick. I gestured to some bubble tea too, which was popular in Mong Kok. I handed over the correct amount of money without much trouble and then shuffled out of the way of the crowds behind me. As I walked away, my first whiff of a stinging smell that I later identified as stinky tofu reached my nose. Aside from the aroma of sweat in the summertime, stinky tofu is the smell of Mong Kok.

I wandered along and munched on my snacks, dipping the long toothpick into the crinkly brown paper to capture the spongy balls. They turned out to be fish balls, though I was not entirely sure whether they contained real fish or not. I decided they were not my favorite things in the world, but I didn't want to turn my nose up at local food. They were basically like rubbery, fish-flavored tofu. I strolled along trying to be open-minded, forcing myself to finish each slimy bite, being jostled by people on all sides. Next, I punctured the top of my cup of bubble tea, which was just regular milk tea swimming with big tapioca balls. It was not the fruity incarnation of bubble tea I had tried back home. That's what I got for not looking carefully enough at the pictures on the menu. The tea was cool, but not cold, and too milky and bland for my taste. The slimy tapioca balls popped up the thick straw one at a time, filling my mouth with gel.

I finished half of the tea and all of the fish balls, then threw away my greasy wrappers and turned toward the Ladies Market for more shopping. The Ladies Market was a long street of stalls that stretched much of the length of Mong Kok. Behind the stalls there were more layers of shops in buildings that formed a pedestrian corridor. At the market they sold everything from fake designer bags, watches, and touristy knick-knacks to lotions and herbal remedies to hospital scrubs and Halloween costumes. If you walked far enough into the depths of the market, you could even find stalls hung with cheap lingerie and rubber sex toys. The Ladies Market had clothes for old ladies, young women, babies, and even for men. I didn't need any clothes, but I did need a cheap watch.

I hoped I wouldn't have to bargain. I hated confrontation, but also did not want to be taken for a tourist. I lived here now; I wanted to find good deals like a local. After ambling through the stalls and looking at my choices amidst the sunglasses and fake jewelry, I found a watch and paid 25 Hong Kong dollars for it, which is about 3.50 USD. The tired, middle-aged woman at the table half-heartedly tried to get me to buy two more for 20 HKD each.

After that I browsed and admired the clothes, bags, and knick-knacks. The market had its fair share of women proclaiming their wares, but they did not hassle me or grab my arms trying to get me to buy things, so it was quite peaceful. Alone in the middle of the crowd, for once I was not lonely. I wandered through the stalls, shoppers, and gawking tourists, getting acquainted with this new type of life. It was good to know that this was not just a quick visit. I could come back here any time. This wasn't some vacation; this was my life. A little painting of an old Chinese boat caught my eye. It would make a nice gift for my older sister, who was teaching English in South Korea.

As I approached the final stalls of the Ladies Market, my phone rang. I almost didn't hear it as the sounds of the street traffic permeated the pedestrian market.

"How's everything going there, are you alright?" Ben said.

"Oh yeah, I'm fine." I slowed to examine a row of knock-off designer purses.

"Are you sure? Are you feeling lonely?" He sounded concerned.

"Actually, I've had a really good day. I'm in Mong Kok—"

"You're in Mong Kok? That's not the safest spot in Hong Kong," he interrupted. When I visited him in Hong Kong before, he had asked me not to venture into Kowloon alone while he was at work.

"I'm being careful and keeping my bag close and all of that. Really, you know that Hong Kong is one of the safest cities in the world. I won't get pulled into a dark alley or anything." I turned around and started slowly making my way back through the market.

"I know, but there was a case of someone throwing acid on people from the windows in Mong Kok."

"I read about that! They caught that guy, so it's all good." The chances were slim that I would actually be the collateral damage of a random act of violence like that when there were so many people around me.

"I worry about leaving you there alone."

"It's not like it's the first time I've ever been to Mong Kok. You did show me around last time. I went to that computer mall and got a portable hard drive, and then I got a watch and a gift for my sister. I've been having a great time." I was proud of myself for traveling off of Hong Kong Island on my own, far from the safe havens of Central and my school's neighborhood.

"That sounds really good actually. Wish I was there with you."

"Aw, I wish you were here, too. We would have had a really nice time wandering the streets together. How's London?"

"Cold and gloomy. I got too used to the warmth in Hong Kong."

I did my best to be cheery, but inside I wanted to grab his hands and drag him through the phone line to be with me. "You're just adjusting, but I'm sure you'll be happy eventually. Remember when you first got to Hong Kong last year? You said there wasn't much to do and it wasn't your favorite place, but you ended up having a good year. You'll rediscover the things you like about London, too."

"Meh, I guess so. What do you have going on this evening?" We chatted as I meandered back through the streets. I made a huge circle around the MTR station before finally noticing where I was. I didn't mention to Ben that I got lost. No need to make him worry.

That night, I went out to dinner by myself. The young Chinese waiter gave me a sympathetic look when I said, "Table for one." I ordered and watched the life around me without the distractions of a companion. A very old woman outside was pushing a cart piled high with cardboard boxes up the steep street. Two women who spoke with Greek accents came into the restaurant. A group of young couples at the table behind me chattered in Cantonese.

As I dined, I noticed other solo diners. In the past, I always went to sit-down restaurants with friends or family, so I didn't notice the other lonely people. Suddenly, I saw them everywhere. They read the newspaper, drank wine or draft beer, and kept a cell phone on the table in case someone called. There were business travelers, old women, solitary backpackers, and even a few young women like me. This was a city where people were comfortable on their own. I was living modern city life, where people were often far from home, busy, and hungry.

A sense of exhilaration drummed through me. I was literally thousands of miles away from all of the closest people in my life. I had gone to university far away from home, but this was a new level of independence and crowded isolation. It reminded me of the first long distance drive I made by myself: eight hours from Los Angeles to Phoenix, speeding through the city traffic and across the desert with the windows down, music of my choice on the radio. I was in complete control. Now, I had the freedom to explore every nook and cranny and random little restaurant. I had the chance to really get to know the intimacies of the Hong Kong streets.

6

CULTURE SHOCK

With my newfound confidence, I explored further afield. Hong Kong was always changing around me. Restaurants went in and out of business with draconian speed. In the last two years I had seen half a dozen restaurants and two grocery stores close their doors in my hometown, and nothing replaced them. The American economy was squeezed tight, and very few people were willing to take risks on new ventures. In Hong Kong it was different; I watched new businesses cropping up all the time and there was always something new to discover.

Hong Kong had thrived in the changing and globalizing world. International influences poured into the city, bringing restaurants and products from every part of the world. 'Authentic Hong Kong cuisine' did not just mean dim sum. This was not merely a process of Westernization. The food culture was just as influenced by Japanese and Indian food as it was by American and European cuisine. The imported tastes had morphed to form the fabric of Hong Kong culture. It was a true melting pot of nations, and as I walked the streets I heard myriad languages pouring from a global assortment of restaurants and shops.

Even so, Hong Kong's culture went deeper than its commerce, and there were rules to follow. It took me a while to figure out what they were. My first embarrassing cultural miscommunication was in a massage parlor.

I'd never had a massage before. They are expensive in the US, seemingly the domain of trophy wives on TV and country club members—not ordinary middle class twenty-somthings. But services in Asia are famously cheap, and massage services are no exception. There seem to be infinite variations. In Hong Kong you could find it all: regular back and body massages, foot massages, massages with oil, massages with hot stones, Thai massages, massages with suction cups, massages with razor blades, massages with happy endings, massages where tiny fish eat the dead skin off your feet (it tickles when they swim between your toes), and the most popular: foot reflexology, designed to assuage all your bodily ills through your feet.

Ben frequently went for foot massages when he worked in Hong Kong, and always recommended it as the ultimate affordable guilty pleasure. I wasn't keen on getting that physically intimate with strangers, but you don't move to Asia every day, so I decided to channel my new enthusiasm and try a massage. I found my way to Ben's favorite place, a dimly lit parlor up a narrow flight of stairs off Elgin Street in Soho.

The shop was warm and cozy, with the distinct smell of lotion and nail polish remover in the air, mixed with a hint of cinnamon. A line of overstuffed chairs filled the wall beside the reception desk. A solitary woman sat reading a fashion magazine with her tiny feet propped up on a padded stool. Feeling self-conscious about my huge American feet, I decided to get a full body massage instead. I indicated my preference on a laminated list of services in English. One of the women working in the parlor handed me a pair of stretchy boxer shorts and directed me to the little side room where a linoleum green massage table and fluffy white towels awaited me.

She closed the door behind her, giving me a chance to change. This was the part that I'd been dreading. In every movie or TV show I'd seen where someone gets a massage, they are left topless with only a towel over their middle third. So, I took my clothes off. It made me feel uncomfortable that a complete stranger was about to spend 40 minutes caressing me, but I kept telling myself, "You're experiencing another culture. You have to do it right, damn it!" I removed everything but the boxer shorts and quickly hopped onto the table so my front was safely covered. I waited for the woman to return.

The door opened and I lifted my head. The woman gave a little jump and her eyes hit the floor. "T-shirt missy? You need?"

"Erm, I'm okay."

"T-shirt?"

"Umm, no thanks?"

"Okaaaay, you have pain?"

"Um, no, maybe just generally across my back?"

She gave me a red-faced smile and set to work on my shoulders. I began to realize that I had done something wrong. I hoped she wouldn't notice my ears becoming pinker than normal and the embarrassed tension in my back. We didn't speak and I tried valiantly not to think about the fact that I was apparently not supposed to be naked for this massage.

I tried to relax and listen to the sounds of the city outside. The room was dark and small, but the slatted windows let in the noise from Elgin Street below. I listened to the foreigners talking and laughing as they wandered in and out of the bars and restaurants. I thought about what the life of a massage lady in this area must be like, always serving those who made the most of her cheap labor by indulging in a luxury they could not afford regularly in their own countries.

When she had me turn over to do the other side of my shoulders she helped me maneuver a towel so I could maintain some semblance of decency. For the remaining minutes she kneaded the tension out of my body as the blood rose in my face. Finally the massage was over and she left the room, saying, "You change now, missy, okay?"

I paid and bolted out the door.

"So, how was your massage?" Ben asked on the phone later.

"Well, it was pretty good. I got the full-body massage. Umm, do you know if you're supposed to, you know, take off your top for those sorts of things?"

"No, I don't think so. The Chinese aren't really comfortable with nudity."

"But in the movies don't people always take off everything?!"

"You didn't strip for your massage, did you?" he said.

"Well, yes! I've never had one before. The lady gave me a pair of boxer shorts and left the room so I thought that's all I was supposed to wear." Maybe I did have a lot in common with Chinese culture. I'd have been much more comfortable staying fully clothed.

Ben laughed and laughed. "You probably made that poor lady really uncomfortable."

"Great, thanks. At least I can chalk it up to being an ignorant foreigner. I am never going back there again."

7

PRACTICE TEACHING

"Good morning, class!"

The students leapt from their little stools. "Good morning, Miss Young!" They bowed and then sat back down, the boys jostling each other for the blue stools, the girls fiddling with their Hello Kitty pencil cases.

"What is the name of this letter?" I asked, holding up a laminated card. A dozen tiny hands flew into the air.

"Beee!"

"Very good! What is the sound of this letter?"

"Beee!"

"The name of the letter is 'be', the sound of the letter is 'buh,'" I would explain, pacing back and forth in front of the upturned faces. "Let's read the words together."

"Balls are bouncing buh buh buh! Balls are bouncing buh buh buh."

"Very good!" I stuck the 'B' card on the long whiteboard with a magnet and pulled off another one, pointing to the letter above a picture of dancing dogs. "What is the name of this letter?"

"Deee!" And so it would go…

The low stools were arranged in three straight rows in front of the whiteboard. The classroom was big, with space for four large tables where the students did their worksheets. There was a bookshelf in the corner filled with boxes of little readers, anywhere from ten to 150 copies of each title. Foam squares covered the floor in the corner like puzzle pieces, with a big red sign saying "Reading Corner" on the wall. On the opposite side of the room, the Computer Corner boasted three desktop monitors that were never used and a screen with a big projector for PowerPoint presentations. Colorful posters full of English words covered the walls, and laminated alphabet cards marched across the top of the whiteboard.

When the students filed into the English room, their bright eyes would range around this space, which was so different from the square rooms with desks in straight lines that populated the rest of the school. The kids were always excited when they came to my class, whispering to each other and giggling as I towered over them. The room, the colors, even each other, provided ample opportunities for their attention to wander. They ranged in age from six to nine years old, and the younger they were the more excited they were about English class. They were smaller on average than American kids of their age, which made them seem especially young and precocious to me.

There was a steep learning curve in my classes—and I'm not talking about the kids. I spent the first class establishing rules like "listen" and "be kind." The kids gave me blank stares and confused giggles in return. I quickly discovered that my students' English level was lower than I had anticipated. I'd had the mistaken impression that everyone in Hong Kong learns English to near fluency early on because of the region's longstanding ties to Great Britain and its mandatory twelve years of English instruction. I thought it would be more like teaching kids back home. Instead, we had to start at the beginning with sounds and one-syllable words.

It took me a few weeks to realize that when I said, "be quiet," they didn't understand what I meant. They had learned the phrase "*keep* quiet" from their teachers, and it was the only command that got a response. They had a difficult time distinguishing between "How are you?"—used by half of the teachers—and "How are you today?"—used by the other half. And the most common mix-up: "How old are you?"

"I'm fine, thank you."

Cantonese is a tonal language, so the students were used to recognizing words by the specific nuances of the sounds. If I said an English word in a different tone of voice or changed the emphasis in a sentence, the students heard the difference and assumed it was a new word. Every day, I had to remind myself to speak slowly and make sure my words were getting through.

I co-taught all my classes with the local English teachers, so I was almost never alone with the kids. It wouldn't be safe to leave such young children with someone who could not understand them if something went wrong. We would divide the classes of 28 students into two groups. "Strawberry group, please stand up. Go to the reading corner. Apple group, please stand up. Go with Miss Wong." They pushed and shoved and laughed as they moved from one area of the classroom to another, chattering in birdlike Cantonese. I would sit down in a little chair and set up a big storybook on a stand as my co-teacher did the same in another corner of the room. We would read the story, pointing out the title, asking the kids to find things in the pictures, and asking questions about the story and vocabulary words.

The main objectives of my classes were to teach reading skills, expose the kids to native English, and encourage them to enjoy the study of the language. I sang songs and played games, but focused on the storybooks. I tried to infuse every lesson with enthusiasm to keep them engaged.

"What is the title? Jenny?" I asked. A little girl in a perfectly pressed blue uniform pointed silently to the words on the cover.

"Very good. What color is the shirt?" I called on the little boy whose hand shot into the air first.

"Blue! It is blue," he said proudly.

"Yes, excellent, Jacky! How many monkeys are there?"

"Five!" the entire group called out together.

"Who can read this sentence? Oscar? How about you?"

One of my other duties was to play English games with the kids at lunch recess. I got out rhyming puzzles, board games or big cardboard dice and spent time chatting with the kids as we played. It was fun to see their confidence grow as they got used to talking to the "foreign teacher." Most of them didn't have any opportunities to practice English outside of school and they enjoyed the novelty of interacting with me.

One of the little boys, who was six years old, always had a particularly bright smile for me. Every time he saw me he shouted, "Miss Young!" and ran over to grab my hand. When we first met he could only say, "How are you today?" and "I'm fine, thank you." I'm not sure he knew what those phrases meant.

"Miss Young!" he would call as he skipped over to me.

"Good morning."

"How are you today?"

"I'm fine, thank you. How are you?"

"I'm fine thank you!"

Every time I tried to teach him something new he would shout, "Yes!" laugh, and then launch into one of his two favorite phrases. "I'm fine thank you how are you today!" His name was Choi Sze Hin, and when I tried to ask him his English name (all the kids had one) he would say, "Choi Sze Hin, how are you today?" I just loved him.

Choi Sze Hin, like many of the students, showed signs of tooth decay. There were black marks between all of his little teeth. I could see them every time he flashed his sweet smile. Most of the kids were from poorer families, and they probably lived with their parents, siblings, and even their grandparents in apartments that were smaller than mine. They wore uniforms, so it was not immediately obvious what kind of families they came from, but their teeth suggested the truth.

Despite the low English level of most of the students, it was still not clear to me why the previous NET had left in such a hurry. The school seemed nice. I still felt a bit isolated, but the students were lovely and no one had been actively unpleasant. The principal, Mr. Tsang, mostly left me to my own devices, but I often saw him joking with the senior teachers and sitting with the kids at recess. He was far less authoritarian than I'd read Hong Kong principals could be. Helen had even told me that he wasn't like other Hong Kong principals. So what was the problem?

8

ROOTS

Taxis formed a dense rim around the old police compound outside my apartment window during rush hour, but the courtyard was still. I had been conjuring up images in my mind of the dastardly deeds that could be taking place inside it. Every once in a while I had noticed a chair in a different place in the courtyard, or a pile of rubbish that hadn't been there before. What if there were triads about? Hong Kong was playing on my imagination. It felt like the sort of place where exciting things happened all the time. It was exotic and romantic, full of fire dragons and cavernous bits of history.

While staring absent-mindedly at the police compound one evening in early October, I got a shock. There was a light on. Someone was there. I climbed onto my window ledge and peered down into the courtyard.

A warm, yellow glow flooded from a window on the ground floor of the building. It was there the next night too, and the one after that. Someone lived there. I wondered what it would be like to have a huge former police station and prison to yourself. Was it spooky? If I lived in a big old police station with a prison out back, I would be scared. There was an appealing thrill of mystery as I watched the light coming on in that corner room. It was a place of unanswered questions. It was a piece of Hong Kong that seemed private, like I was the only person who watched it from above. I had moved to Ben's hometown, but it felt important to make pieces of it my own, to discover secrets he didn't know that I might be able to show him someday.

But Ben was *not* the only connection I had to Hong Kong before moving. My dad was born here.

My grandpa, Keith Young, was the son of small-town dairy farmers on the southern Oregon coast. He took off for the wide world as soon as he could, serving on a US Navy ship in the South Pacific during World War II and then working for the military's dairy supplier. My grandma, Donna, finished college in Ohio and left—like I did—to teach abroad. She taught the children of American servicemen in Hawaii and Japan, where she met my grandpa. He was older than the soldiers who courted her teacher friends—and he had a car. He bought her a gift for every one of their dates during their year-long courtship, and asked her to marry him half a dozen times. By the time she was ready to say yes, he'd given up and she had to ask him. Shortly after their little wedding, thousands of miles from their families, they moved to Hong Kong.

My grandparents were stationed in Hong Kong, Thailand, Korea, and the Philippines before they finally retired and returned to America the year I was born. They built a house on the Oregon coast and filled it with mementos of their lives in Asia. Throughout my childhood, I spent a few weeks a year in their home decorated with Buddhas and Hindu gods, Filipino fabrics, rosewood tables, carvings of caribou, Thai elephants, Japanese dishes and scrolls full of beautiful Chinese calligraphy. My grandparents didn't stop traveling. They sent us postcards from Europe, emails from freighter cruises on the Mediterranean, and stories from a world that always showed them more corners to explore.

I wondered what Hong Kong must have been like for a young couple starting their lives together, full of the excitement of a brand new relationship and a foreign land. Would the Western influences have been as visible? Did they truly feel like they were living in China back then? I didn't. Whatever Hong Kong was, it didn't feel quite like China.

I had visited my grandparents the summer before I left for Hong Kong, asking for more stories. "I thought you might like to see these," my grandma said one evening as I sat at the kitchen counter admiring a mango wood bowl from Thailand. "I saved copies of all our annual letters for you kids, in case you'd like to see a bit of our history." She had faithfully written detailed Christmas letters home to the US throughout the 30 years that they lived abroad.

"I'd love to have them!"

I pulled the yellowed cards, perfectly organized, from the bottom of the stack. The first letter, marked with the heading "Hong Kong, BCC, Christmas, 1955," described the beginning of their international romance.

As most of you know, a little over a year ago on an island in the Pacific, at the fringe of the Orient, a certain bachelor and an almost-old-maid-schoolteacher met and formed a friendship which, in a matter of months, mushroomed into a courtship. I don't think anyone was as bewildered by the swift course of events that then took place as the two involved. Friends afterward remarked that they "knew it all the time". To be as brief as possible, the sudden news of a transfer of the bachelor brought about the realization that the two would certainly be parted. Nothing would do but to change the long-standing status of each—to take that "fatal" step. (1955)

They were married by an Army chaplain in Okinawa and awaited the news of where my grandpa would be transferred next. It must have taken courage to marry someone you had known for barely a year, not knowing where in the world your journey together would take you. Ben and I had done the safe thing, not wanting to take that "fatal step" without spending ample time together in the same country first. We were willing to be parted for a season. Had the world changed so much, or were we just less romantic than that bachelor and almost-old-maid-schoolteacher? Maybe Ben and I should have gotten married so we could be together no matter what, like my grandparents. Fifty-six years of marriage, plus four kids and seventeen grandkids, had proved they made the right choice. And of course, their decision brought them to Hong Kong.

In early August we prepared ourselves to leave at a moment's notice, and were ready when Keith was called in by Mr. Murphy, supervisor of all plants in the Far East. His announcement that we were to go to Hong Kong, if we were agreeable, came as a complete surprise to all concerned, especially us. It took us only a few minutes to decide, for it meant a definite promotion for Keith—and, well, who would refuse an offer to live in fabulous Hong Kong? (1955)

Who indeed? I knew how pleased my grandparents were that my romance had taken me to this strange island too.

Actually, Hong Kong is a wonderful place to live—we think. Of course there are many things one could complain about, as there are wherever you go, but we think there are far more things to enjoy and be thankful for. The price of food is very high, and apartments are quite expensive. As Keith puts it, most necessities are costly, yet luxuries, cheap. One luxury we still glory in having is an amah, or Chinese servant. They live very cheaply; therefore their services can be bought at a ridiculously low price. Too, Hong Kong is a wonderful place to shop. It is an open port, and therefore a city of traders. Beautiful things from all over the world can be bought here tax-free, in most cases. Tourists who stop here with any money at all usually go home with empty pockets, but suitcases filled with jade, tailor-made clothes bought for half the prices at home, ivory ornaments and jewelry, or most anything your imagination might conceive. We just love living here, and are sure it will be a long time before we become bored with it, if ever. (1955)

It seemed that despite the addition of an entirely new skyline, the essence of Hong Kong hadn't changed much in those 55 years. The shopping was still legendary and the luxuries were still cheap. These days, the newly wealthy came from Mainland China to buy tax-free luxury designer items and property. Tourists still left with full suitcases and lighter wallets. Most of the domestic helpers were no longer Chinese, but Filipino and Indonesian. They kept Hong Kong people supplied with home-cooked meals and wrinkle-free shirts for about 450 USD per month. Even the teachers at my school had full-time, live-in help.

I turned over another card, dated Christmas, 1956, which featured a picture of a chubby, black-haired baby wearing a little silk outfit and a round Chinese hat with a queue attached—my dad. I looked at the next card. It had a picture of the same little boy in the same Chinese hat, with an even chubbier baby brother sitting beside him in a wicker chair. The card from 1959 showed three little boys in matching silk outfits. In 1960, a Chinese junk boat joined the family, pictured with its old-fashioned sails unfurled in the harbor breeze. By 1961, the three little boys had a baby sister. The letters inside the cards overflowed with tales of family life surrounded by the mystery of Hong Kong.

We are firmly convinced that there cannot possibly be any other place like it! It is a city where anything can be done, and usually is. However, there is no such thing as convention. The best attitude to assume is to expect anything, and count on nothing. There is a very definite informality and easy-goingness in life here, and the Chinese people themselves are imperturbable and unbothered. The person used to the highly-geared life in the states has need to learn to adjust to the different, and sometimes erratic, pace – and also to learn to count to one hundred rather than to ten. If he can do this successfully, he is bound to enjoy life in Hong Kong. (1956)

As I turned the pages of each letter from 1955 to 1962, I entered a world that was similar but in some ways drastically different from my own Hong Kong. I knew that life here was now just as highly geared as, if not more than, life in the states. I'd discovered that the only answer my co-workers gave when I asked about their days was "so busy!" But it was still true that anything can be done in Hong Kong, and usually is.

My grandma's descriptions of her life were filled with babies and her adjustments to working with the Chinese amahs. I found that I related more to the brief references to my grandpa's work. He was one of just two foreigners at the dairy plant he managed; I now knew well what it was like to work in an entirely different culture. However, his conclusions surprised me.

Keith continues to find his job a most interesting one, and always challenging. Working with Chinese labor is understandably a far different experience than any that might be encountered in the dairy field at home. There are always things to learn and so many more to strive for. The standards of efficiency are much higher in the states, yet the bases for the standards are very unlike those here. Keith finds each day one that is not only full, but with opportunities. (1956)

After my short months in Hong Kong I had discovered that this country was jaw-droppingly efficient. The trains in the MTR always arrived on time, and if you missed one another would be along in three minutes flat. Plumbers and cable guys always turned up when they said they would, and most bureaucratic tasks could be completed in no time at all. You could pay your electricity bill at an ATM, and even paying taxes was easier: you could fill out a return online in ten minutes. The Hong Kong airport was recognized as one of the very best in the world; it was clean and efficient and going through security took less than five minutes. As life became increasingly cumbersome and worrying in the

US, I was discovering a city that had leapt ahead into the future, far further than my grandparents could ever have imagined back then.

As my grandma's passion for her new city and her new life poured from the pages of the brittle old letters, her excitement was infectious. She had a longstanding passion for learning new things and experiencing as much of the world as she could. I found common ground and comfort in the old words. I was thankful that her love for strange places had found its way to me.

9

CO-TEACHING

*We are coming to learn more and more about the Chinese people—
Keith, through the men at work, and I, through the amahs here at
home. They are an interesting people with ways that are often very
difficult to change. When it comes to a difference in ideas between the
East and the West as to how things are to be done, there is often heard
a saying which is common among the Americans here: "They won this
battle 3000 years ago!" As is true whenever peoples of different cultures
meet, each must do his share of adapting. How happy one is in Hong
Kong is very largely dependent upon the degree to which he is able to
adjust. So far, we're holding up fine! (1957)*

I was learning first-hand what it's like to work side by side with people
from another culture. Despite all the time I'd spent being in love with
a Hong Kong man, it didn't help me understand the people as much as
I thought it would. His had been an international, affluent upbringing,
with regular trips abroad and many years in English boarding schools and
universities. My co-workers had grown up in regular families in Hong
Kong and the Mainland, and their exposure to other cultures was—at
times—limited.

The local teachers taught English through rote repetition and dictation,
a practice that was very different from most Western language classes,
which rely heavily on conversation activities. Dictation and repetition are
essential if you are trying to learn Chinese characters, so why shouldn't

they teach other languages the same way? In practice, it had become more important for the kids to answer questions accurately on the worksheets and exams than to communicate in the new language. I guessed this was how a few of the teachers could become English teachers without really being able to speak English comfortably. They taught the textbook and they taught to the tests, but many lacked the confidence to converse. June, the teacher who sat next to me, once went to New Zealand for a professional development course and the school she visited displayed a sign that said, "Mistakes are okay." June told us, "This was one of the cultural differences that I noticed." In Hong Kong schools, mistakes were not okay, even if making them helped you to learn.

The other English teachers and I had regular co-planning meetings in which we were supposed to design lessons together. During the first few months of school, as Helen had instructed me to, I carefully saved drafts of my lesson ideas on the shared computer drive in advance so we could fine-tune them together. The teachers of, say, Primary 2 would gather around a table in the staffroom, textbooks and planners stacked in front of them. I'd speak about my idea in general terms, being careful not to dictate exactly how the lesson would go. I didn't want to make it sound like I, the outsider, the newcomer, the Westerner, was telling them how to run things in their school. I'd ask whether anyone had any suggestions or problems with the plan. Invariably, they stared blankly back at me. Miss Wong would play with her pen. Mr. Zhou's eyes, and then his head, would droop. Then they'd open their textbooks and move on to the Cantonese portion of the meeting. I was dismissed.

After a few awkward weeks, I realized the teachers were not reading the plans on the shared drive at all, so I printed out copies for everyone and spelled out the class activities in more detail during the meetings. "Does this sound okay to you? Do you have any other ideas for the post-reading activity?" Still, no one would say anything. I wondered if they were concerned with saving face, either for me or themselves. Did they not want to speak up to avoid contradicting me? Were they worried about looking bad? Maybe they were just happy that they didn't have to prepare anything for our classes.

Helen was my guardian angel. She always had good ideas for her students, and she was also the most comfortable speaking English during meetings. At first, she was my only collaborator. One teacher made it pretty clear that he thought my lessons were a waste of time. Mr. Liu routinely brought his students to class late, and often sat in the back of the room grading papers or making a few kids do extra worksheet corrections instead of co-teaching with me. Every once in a while, he would stand up to shout at a few of the whispering kids, and then he'd go right back to grading.

We got off on the wrong foot from the beginning. This was the very same teacher who I'd asked if it was his first year teaching. Maybe I had made him lose face by suggesting he was inexperienced. One thing was certain: he hadn't liked me since then. Mr. Liu sat diagonally from me in the staff room, and Helen and June had their cubicles on either side of mine. Helen, June, and I always greeted each other in the mornings. I tried saying good morning to Mr. Liu every day for weeks, but he never responded. Eventually I resorted to pasting on a broad smile whenever I walked past him.

The odd thing was that he never referred to me by name. Most of the teachers couldn't say my first name because of the double 'n' sound in Shannon. It usually came out sounding like Shallin or Sharon. The teachers who didn't speak much English called me Miss Young. Mr. Liu, on the other hand, called me "NET Teacher" when he talked to other people and did not call me anything when he spoke to me directly. To get my attention from across the cubicle wall he'd make a strange, whispering "ssspssssst" sound.

Apart from Mr. Liu, the atmosphere in the teacher's office was cheery, but busy. By now most of the teachers greeted me with a nod in the morning. Sometimes I tried to make conversation:

"Hi Miss Lo. How's it going?"

"I am going to the library."

"Ah."

They loved it when I spoke Cantonese, saying "*jo san*" instead of "good morning." I'd usually get a laugh and a smile for my trouble. For the rest of the day they ran around, textbooks in hand, and many of them stayed late to grade. They always seemed to be far busier than me. I tried to alleviate their burden by preparing all the resources for our classes, and I tried to be flexible.

"Miss Young, the exams are in two weeks, and the teachers would like to take back your lessons for review," Helen would say to me every few months.

I had fourteen classes that I taught once each week. "How many do they need?"

"Two or three for each class, okay?"

"Okay, I guess that's fine. So the next class I'll teach will be when?"

"After the school holiday."

"Right."

When my classes were co-opted for exam review, I was left feeling frustrated. My work was clearly secondary to the all-important examinations. Never was I asked to help prepare the students for the exams. Never was I expected to grade essays, or even workbooks. My classes were a box to check; each kid needed their share of time with the NET. It was hard to feel fulfilled at work when my contributions seemed to go against the grain, or worse, to be irrelevant. I wanted to get to London to start what I hoped would be my real career, a career filled with books and authors and lunch dates with Ben.

I made plans during a long weekend to visit my sister, Chelsea, who had been teaching English in Korea for nearly two years. Even though Korea is a four-hour flight from Hong Kong, as far as Washington State is from Arizona, it felt like we were neighbors. I was eager to find out how she was handling the cultural differences, whether she sometimes also felt out of step with everyone else.

When my co-workers found out I was going to Korea, they surprised me: "Koreans can be very pushy," said Miss Lo.

"Yes, a very angry country," said one of the Floras.

"The food is not so good as Hong Kong."

"I like the shopping and in Korea it is not good shopping like Japan, only cheaper."

I was surprised at how blunt everyone was. The Americans I knew (with some unfortunate exceptions) were apologetic about their prejudices, often choosing to pretend they didn't exist or speak them behind closed doors. My co-workers were not shy about sharing their judgments. If they thought someone—themselves and their friends included—was too fat or too ugly, they would say so. Jenny, one of the nicest teachers at the school, once told me she was "so fat!" I didn't know how to respond when another teacher told me she liked me specifically because she thought I was young and pretty (not because I was a good teacher). An American might think that, but would never say it. The teachers would even announce which students they thought were stupid and which ones were clever—within the hearing of the children! This was an aspect of the culture, or at least my school's culture, that I found very difficult to get used to.

10

SOUTH KOREA

When the long weekend arrived, I headed straight to the airport from my school, suitcase in tow. There was an added bonus to this trip: I was going to meet Chelsea's own international love interest. Enter Francois: tall, smart, South African accent. He was Chelsea's co-teacher at the private kindergarten where she worked—and he'd quickly become her serious boyfriend. It was already time to assess his brother-in-law potential.

As I boarded the plane, I thought back to the first time Chelsea met Ben. She had spent a semester in London at the same time as me, though on a different program. We all went out for Thai food together, and Ben chose that moment to regale us with a tale of how his Chinese mum, who I had not yet met, would judge me based on my looks. I'd listened in horror as he elaborated on her high standards, on how she'd say it to my face if she didn't think I was pretty enough for him. I waited, as I'm sure Chelsea did too, for him to say, "but of course I'd go out with you anyway" or "but you're much too pretty to worry about that."

He didn't give any such reassurances.

I confronted him about it in private after dinner. He was surprised. "I thought it went without saying that you're more than pretty enough."

"You didn't say that."

"You know I think you're beautiful. It didn't need to be said."

"That was my big sister! It needed to be said." The blood rushed in my ears. Couldn't he see how important this was?

"It makes a way better story when it sounds more extreme," Ben said.

"You're not going for a good story! You should have been worrying about making a good impression as a boyfriend, not telling a good story!"

It was our first fight. He'd apologized, but I worried that the damage was done. Without a love interest of her own at the time, Chelsea was in a position to be particularly critical of Ben, and her wariness of him had lasted. They had never really clicked.

It went slightly better the first time Ben met the rest of my family. They got along well—just without me.

We had planned to fly to Arizona on the same day: me from my college in New York and Ben from London. But travel delays in snow-bound Syracuse and a gate delay caused me to miss my connection in Atlanta. It was the last flight of the night. Meanwhile, Ben's flight from London arrived right on time. My parents picked him up from the airport and kept him entertained while I fretted and fumed in an airport hotel. I made it there the next day at noon. That's when I learned that my mom had accidentally closed the car door on Ben's hand when they picked him up from the airport. She felt terrible about it, but he was very gracious. My siblings had been the ones to tattle to me. Fortunately, my family liked him—though my siblings pointed out that he used a lot of swear words.

Now it was my turn to be the concerned sister.

I touched down in Korea and wandered around the clean, modern Seoul International Airport until Chelsea and Francois found me. After an enthusiastic greeting from Chelsea and the presentation of Francois, I was introduced to their baby, Matiz.

Matiz was a cheap little Korean car that Chelsea and Francois bought together. Matiz's primary purpose was to deliver them to the beach, but she also carried groceries from time to time. We collected some Korean snacks ("You have to try Peppero!") and then sped along the highway, watching the lights of Seoul. The buildings were not quite as tall and close together as the ones in Hong Kong. We crossed a bridge and curved around the city toward their town: Suwon. Chelsea and I talked as quickly as we drove, with occasional commentary from Francois in the driver seat. By the time Matiz drove into Suwon it was dark. I had a brief impression of low buildings and miniature streets lined with miniature cars like the one we were in.

The air had a crisp feeling that had not made it south to Hong Kong yet. We unloaded the groceries they had picked up on the way to the airport and walked through an empty park to a popular beer and fries shop that had a whopping seventeen dipping sauces. "We've tried almost all of them," Francois said. "It's one of our favorite places." We picked up the very last order of steaming fries before the shop ran out for the night and sat down to eat them at plastic picnic tables outside. Groups of young, hip Koreans hung around, laughing raucously. The street had a friendly, neighborhood atmosphere and I felt immediately at ease.

Chelsea and I swapped stories about home, and Francois laughed along with us. He'd heard enough stories about our family to be able to talk naturally about the brothers and sisters he'd never met. He had a laid-back, nonjudgmental way of speaking. He was a good match for Chelsea's talkative, opinionated personality—always the opposite of mine. I noticed they were not shy about holding hands and rubbing shoulders in front of me, like I hadn't been able to do with Ben. I envied the closeness that they had shared in the past year.

Chelsea and Francois's relationship was the polar opposite of my life with Ben. They worked together, socialized together, cooked together, traveled together. They didn't live together, but they were always close, getting to know each other better every day. Ben and I lived in different countries, saw each other only through a computer screen, sometimes ate meals together on Skype, and spoke about trips we would take together some day. We'd been through more life changes during our relationship:

college, graduation, first jobs, international moves. But in their one-year relationship they'd had about as much time physically together as Ben and I had in three!

"So, I know it's early to ask this," Chelsea said as soon as we were alone on the first night, "but what do you think of him?" Francois's apartment building was across the street and he had gone home for the evening.

"I like him. He seems friendly and smart. It's nice that he's tall."

She laughed. "I know! I can wear heels around him!"

"You guys seem really comfortable together."

We talked about how their relationship unfolded over their time in Korea, and about my parents' impressions of him. They had visited Korea shortly before I moved to Hong Kong. Chelsea mentioned how good it was to get someone else's perspective of him from people she had known all her life. "It's like my two different lives are coming together."

"Does it worry you that you haven't met his family?"

"I'm a little nervous about that, but hopefully we'll be visiting them in South Africa when our contracts end."

"You're not worried about the cultural differences?"

"I'm sure we'll be fine. They'll be like him, right?"

I thought about when the rest of my family were getting to know Ben. He had a British sense of humor, which they were not used to, and they noticed that he sometimes made jokes that poked fun at me. They were worried that I would end up feeling dismissed or diminished and voiced their concerns. I was surprised at the time; Ben's sense of humor was typical of other British people I'd met. They seemed to use insults to express affection. On the other hand, he also had no problem complimenting me and talking to me about his feelings. I'd never doubted that Ben respected me. His banter was born of his confidence in my own self-assurance. He knew that beneath my sometimes shy exterior, I was tough. It was a quality I didn't think my family always recognized. Never one to crack jokes myself, my siblings didn't pick on me as much as they did on each other. Perhaps they thought I couldn't take it—but Ben had faith in me.

Chelsea and Francois had to work on the first full day I was in Korea. I slept in, and then wandered over to the school to meet them for lunch. The apartments and the school building were close to a university, giving the area a youthful vibe. The apartment buildings were only four to eight stories tall, unlike the 20-plus-story buildings that filled Hong Kong from end to end.

I arrived at the school in time to sit in on one of Chelsea's classes. She introduced me to her students, who had all drawn pictures for me. They were five or six years old, all girls, and completely adorable. They didn't have to wear uniforms, so they were all dressed in pink and purple. There were only four students in the class, and Chelsea said they had been attending English kindergarten for nearly three years now. Their level of English was much better than that of my students: I distinctly heard one of them use the word 'curious' correctly.

Chelsea's job was very different from mine. She had small groups of students and taught all subjects entirely in English. The curriculum and materials were prepared ahead of time, but she taught all day every day. With small groups and large amounts of time, she really got to know her students. Since I only saw my huge groups once a week, I still didn't know the names of all 300 kids.

The school, an affluent private kindergarten, was full of colorful pictures and balloons and tiny chairs and tables. It felt like a fun daycare center, with some school thrown in. In my local Hong Kong school, the students sat in desks like high-schoolers and wore uniforms and stood in perfect lines. However, in both countries and both types of schools, the culture dictated that children must study, study, study so that when they grow up they can work, work, work. These kids would spend half the day at English kindergarten, and then go on to hours more of Korean school, often followed by tutoring and piano lessons. Hong Kong students would do the same.

The other difference between our schools was that Chelsea and Francois had three co-workers who were also native English speakers. As soon as I stepped into the staff office, the camaraderie with their fellow teachers was obvious. They worked with a hipster Canadian couple, Miranda and Gabe, and an American girl called Sarah. They made plans to meet up after work, told stories about their students, complained about their schedules. It reminded me of teaching in the US; I tried not to be jealous.

After a lunch of Korean barbecue and kimchi with Chelsea and Francois, I headed for Hwaseong Fortress, an ancient wall surrounding a large portion of the city of Suwon. A path of rough stone steps led the way up a hill, the wall on one side and the city on the other. Lots of people were out for walks in the sunshine with me. The air was pine-scented and clear, and the sounds of birds filtered through the trees. As I walked, sometimes I was high above the city; sometimes a green park sloped up towards the wall and sometimes a lookout tower or small shrine appeared in front of me. The view from above got better and better. I could see countless rooftops, temples, and even a European-style cathedral from the wall. Guard towers and elaborate gateways broke up the stone circle. The neighborhoods below looked ordinary except for the ancient stone wall rising above them. It was peaceful and solitary. A cool breeze blew over the old stone ramparts, carrying muted sounds from the city below.

When I was about halfway around the city, I decided to splurge on an international roaming call to Ben. "Hey, how are you?"

"I'm alright. How's Korea?" He sounded tired. He had been hard at work in his London office. I reached a tourist area by one of the main gates with a gift shop, snack bar, and a Korean archery range.

"It's pretty cool. I'm having a good time so far. I'm on this big wall and they have a field set up for tourists to do Korean archery."

"Are you going to try it?"

"I don't think it would be as much fun by myself."

"That's probably true, we should do it together sometime."

"Yes, we should! So, what are you up to?"

"Well, I got sent home from work today. I seem to be sick and felt quite dizzy."

"Really? What happened?"

"I think the long hours are catching up with me, and there's a flu going around."

"Aw, I wish I could bring you some chicken soup." I thought about the space of one street that separated Chelsea and Francois and the space of one hemisphere that separated Ben and me.

"What do you think of Francois?" he asked.

"I like him. He's super laid-back." I crossed a bridge as we talked about my visit so far. Water from a canal cascaded over concrete steps below.

Occasionally, other walkers passed me. As I was descending from the highest point of the wall, a Buddhist monk appeared on a narrow section of the path. He carried a walking stick and wore simple sandals on the rough stone. As we neared each other, he gave me the most genuinely friendly smile I had ever seen. It left me feeling cheery and warm as I walked on. The Koreans didn't seem nearly as angry as my co-workers had warned me.

Eventually, Ben had to say goodbye. I continued my solitary march around the ramparts. After two hours, the guard posts, nooks and crannies all looked the same. Near the end of my trek, I found a busy market, not unlike the one in Mong Kok. There were the usual clothes and handbags and kitchen supplies, interspersed with gadgets and gimmicks and groceries. One large section of the market displayed seafood in various shapes and states (living, dead, dried). Another sported fruits and vegetables that were sometimes recognizable and sometimes exotic. I didn't buy anything, but I inhaled the jumbled sights and rough smells.

There were more rotting vegetables and defecating dogs in this market, and I preferred the stinky tofu smell of Mong Kok.

With a few hours left before everyone got off work, I picked random streets and shops to explore. Korea felt more like a European country than I had expected. There seemed to be cute, independent coffee shops on every corner. They had themes, each more original than the last. Chelsea and Francois later told me about one that had songbirds that were free to fly around the café and visit with the patrons.

That night, we met up with Chelsea's co-workers at their favorite quirky bar. We climbed past Phantom of the Opera candles into a dimly lit space filled with low tables and Persian rugs. The walls were made of dripped and baked clay and there were oddities in every corner. Fishing nets hung with eclectic objects were draped from the walls and ceiling. One brushed my forehead as we made our way to an alcove in the back. We sat on big, furry animal skins and ordered wine in old-fashioned jugs.

Chelsea's friends were cool and relaxed. They told stories about their cultural mishaps and frustrations, and about their explorations around Asia. I had missed hanging out with people who spoke my language fluently. They were essentially doing the same thing I was: having an international adventure, chasing the opportunities abroad. Their experiences were similar, their feelings of displacement familiar. It made my isolation in Hong Kong all the more apparent.

The next day Chelsea, Francois and I took the train to Seoul. It rained the entire day, but we bought a couple of umbrellas from 7-Eleven and explored the city anyway, ducking into coffee shops whenever the rain picked up. We went to an ancient palace full of open courtyards, peaked roofs and beautiful painted wood. This sort of architecture was a lot harder to find in Hong Kong. The process of modernization had been so rapid there that most of the traditional buildings were simply gone. The only exceptions were a few Tin Hau temples, heavily clouded with incense and tourists. They hadn't saved many of the Victorian buildings from the British Empire days, except for the old police complex.

Afterwards we explored a shopping mall full of colorful Korean kitsch and a touristy antique street. I found a tiny celadon vase that matched a pair my parents bought when visiting Grandma and Grandpa in Korea. Glazed birds swooped across the curved green porcelain and around the slender neck. The shopkeeper wrapped it carefully in paper and I stowed it in my bag. It would be my little apartment's first decoration.

Upon taking a few steps outside the vase shop, I heard a loud voice coming from a cart in the street. "Step right up! See the magic candy floss. You think it's only one string? Think again!" A young man stood behind the cart, twirling what appeared to be a clump of hardened honey in his hand. "We'll make a loop here, like a donut. You think it is only one loop? Watch the magic happen."

"You have to see this, Shannon," Francois said. We joined the crowd around the cart. The young man dipped the loop into a bowl of flour and twirled it around his hands, continuing his fast-talking presentation. The loop grew larger, thinner. It looked like a ring of supple pizza dough. The young man doubled the ring, dipped it in the flour and continued to swing it around his hands.

"You see two rings now? Just wait. Ready? Four. What's next? Eight. That's right. How many loops do you see now? Sixteen it is." The loops twirled faster as he doubled them around his hands like hair ties, dipping them in the flour each time. He chanted as the dough thinned into strings. "Thirty-two. Know what's next? Sixty-four. Can we do it? One hundred twenty-eight. How many strings do you see? Two hundred fifty-six. One more? Five hundred twelve!" By now the strings were so thin that I thought they must break, but still the man twisted. The crowd cheered him on. "One thousand twenty-four!" He held up the loop of sugar like spun silk. As soon as we had cheered and admired his handiwork, he cut the loop into pieces and wrapped the fine threads around ground peanuts and coconut. He gave each white bundle to the people waiting in the crowd. It was like rich cotton candy with a crunchy center. "Dragon's beard candy!" he announced as we lined up to buy boxes to take home.

"That was amazing!"

Francois smiled. "I knew you'd like it. Wait 'til you try the food at the restaurant tonight. It's one of our favorites."

The steely sky in Seoul turned dark all too soon and before I knew it, it was time to head back to Hong Kong. I nearly missed my flight, not wanting to say goodbye. I waved farewell, missing them both already. They assured me they would visit me in Hong Kong soon.

11

New NETs

In mid-October, I attended an induction course for new NET teachers. They'd come together from local schools across Hong Kong for the four-day session. When I walked into the classroom at an educational facility in the New Territories, I was surprised to find not a room full of globe-trotting recent grads like Chelsea's friends, but dozens of teachers who looked like moms and dads. These were not the teach-abroad backpacking types I had expected (and hoped) to meet here. I scanned the auditorium. There! A group of younger teachers occupied the third row. I crossed my fingers and went over to introduce myself to a girl with bleached blonde hair and multi-colored eyeliner.

"I'm Samantha, from Canada," she said. "Have you heard of Windsor? It's across the border from Detroit."

"I've heard of Detroit."

The girl next to her spoke up. She had a wide smile and was dressed in dark colors. "I'm from Canada too! My family lives near Toronto. I'm Emma." Emma was Chinese, and introduced us to another Chinese girl next to her, Melanie.

"I'm also from Canada," Melanie said.

"I'm so excited to be here!" Sam said. "I just got the call a few weeks ago and we had to pack up and move in a few days. I'm already sick from the pollution though."

"Really? I've been in Hong Kong for almost two months," I said.

"Me too," said Emma. "It's strange they're doing induction so late. I mean, we've already figured out what to do at our schools by now."

"Yeah, my kids are already doing their first exams," I said.

"I guess my school just does everything late. I didn't even know I was supposed to come today until yesterday afternoon," Samantha said, running a hand through her peroxide blonde hair.

"Do you get along well with the other teachers so far?" I asked.

"Yes! They're really nice to me. They took me straight to buy an umbrella when they picked me up at the airport. They said it was for the sun, not the rain!" Sam said, eyes wide.

"My school keeps me really busy so far, just like the local teachers," Emma said. "I don't want them to know I speak a bit of Cantonese or I'll have to go to all the meetings too."

"I have to go to Cantonese meetings anyway, sometimes," I said. That was easily my least favorite part of my job. Helen was good about translating only the parts that were relevant to me, which was usually no more than ten minutes' worth of a three-hour meeting. The rest of the time, I doodled on the handouts (all written in Chinese characters, of course) or stared into space. The other teachers were very sympathetic.

The session began and we watched PowerPoint presentations about how to get settled in Hong Kong. Most of the information was stuff I had already figured out by that time. The presenters lectured us about the difficulties of working in a school system that operated under a different educational philosophy than the West. They warned us to be prepared for the differences. More specifically, they warned us about the exams.

Students in Hong Kong take week-long exams four times a year, starting from primary school when they are barely six years old. They spend hours preparing in class and at tutoring sessions before and after school. In the US, students go to tutoring only if they are struggling, and even then many of them don't bother. In Hong Kong, almost all students go to tutoring so they can be competitive. The tiniest kids have several hours of homework per night.

The students were very good at learning certain types of information, far better than Western students, but the emphasis on creativity and intellectual skepticism I had experienced in my Western education had no place in this system. I had to figure out how to be respectful, but at the same time I could not agree that the endless examinations and after-school tutorial classes were good for kids that age. I worried that the kids wouldn't have enough time to cultivate a love of learning that might get them through high school. Still, the Chinese students were far more focused and dedicated than the kids back home. America could take a few cues from contemporary Chinese culture and put a greater emphasis on the value of education, ideally with a bit of balance. Privately, I resolved to make my lessons extra fun after the exams.

There is tremendous pressure to do well on the exams, the presenters explained. This is a cultural practice that stems from the Chinese civil service exams that could make or break a career in one arduous test. In addition, secondary schools are banded according to their quality. If a student doesn't do well on their primary exams, they will not be able to get into a top-tier Band One secondary school. Their chances at a college education are nearly obliterated by the time they turn twelve if they can't get into a first- or second-tier school. Competition was becoming more fierce even to get into good primary schools. Rather than being allocated places based on where they lived, students had to go to interviews and prepare lengthy applications while they were still in kindergarten. Even the local papers acknowledged that it was getting out of hand.

Because childhood academic performances will affect the rest of their lives, parents in Hong Kong make their children put education above everything, no matter what effects obsessive studying might have on normal childhood development. The presenters told horror stories about primary school students jumping out of windows due to the pressure and children being beaten when they didn't get good exam results. The worst stories all seemed to happen in Tin Shui Wai, the low-income area in the New Territories where Sam worked. Every time a new story was told, Sam would glance over at us and whisper, "That's where we live!" By the end of the session we were all convinced she should move. The information was sobering, but it was yet another puzzle piece that would hopefully help us understand our schools a little better.

On our first break it became clear that I was not the only person whose main reason for attending the induction was to meet people. The coffee and conversation flowed as everyone swapped names and stories. Sam, Emma and I joined a group that had formed near the snack table in the hall.

I dumped sugar in my coffee and listened in. "I went out the other night with some triad guys. It was insane!" said Shane, an ebullient Canadian who had come to Hong Kong with his girlfriend Lauren, also a NET teacher. The triads are the Chinese mafia.

"How did that happen?" someone asked.

Shane launched into the tale, waving his arms as he talked. "So, my buddy invited me out for drinks, right? He was like, 'Hey, Shane! Come along, it'll be great!' and I figured, 'Eh, why not?' so we got to this bar and it was fuckin' crazy. We went down some basement stairs and these tattooed guys were sitting around drinking buckets of beer. And I'm thinking, 'These are fucking triad guys.' They all knew my buddy, but I'm thinking, 'I hope I don't die tonight, man.' And then we got wasted, sitting there with these guys who could have killed us. I didn't get home until about 6 a.m. I was wandering around for an hour trying to find my way through Hong Kong where all the fucking buildings look exactly the same. It was insane!"

"Were you there for all of this?" I asked Lauren, a pretty brunette with a business-like face who seemed to be the common sense in this couple.

"No, I told him you go out on your own, and I'll go to bed early," she said, her strong Canadian accent coming out in the way she said 'out.'

"Yeah… my buddy's into all sorts of shit," Shane continued, "He's been living in China and I guess Hong Kong seems tame to him. It's a far cry from Nova Scotia, that's for sure."

The new teachers were a diverse bunch, mostly hailing from Canada and Australia, with others from the UK, the US, New Zealand, South Africa, Ireland, Singapore, and India. A few came with spouses; a few came to escape the poor economies in their own countries; a few had been teaching English in Asia for a while and Hong Kong was the next stop on the TEFL world tour; a few had already been teaching in tutorial centers in Hong Kong. Most of them were older than the average EFL teacher; the NET job in Hong Kong paid enough to support families and mortgages and typically attracted more experienced teachers. The one thing we had in common was that we were all there for an adventure.

At lunchtime, Sam, Emma and I joined Melanie and another young teacher at one of the tables, our group already established. We dug into our plates of noodles and assorted salads and started brandishing stories about getting started in Hong Kong. Sam had come to Hong Kong after her local economy, inextricably tied to the Detroit auto industry, had tanked. She'd brought along her brand-new fiancé. Emma, too, had struggled to find a permanent teaching job in Canada. Melanie had already been teaching in Hong Kong for a year. It was nice to chat with people who shared my language, and some of my circumstances.

"Have you guys been to Disneyland yet?" asked Samantha. "The Disney princesses live in our building! I saw Sleeping Beauty in the elevator yesterday."

"Not yet," I replied. "I've heard it's pretty small. Ocean Park is supposed to be a lot better."

"Yeah, it's really fun," said Melanie. "I haven't bothered to go to Disneyland."

Emma chimed in. "I totally want to go when my boyfriend comes to visit." She told us she had been dating a guy in Canada for only eight months before she left, and was apprehensive about her new long distance relationship.

"When will he be here?"

"Probably in November. I'm hoping he'll want to stay, but he'd rather work in China. His family is from the Mainland."

"Boy, that's tough. My ex and I did the long distance thing for a while. It didn't work out," said Melanie. "It was too hard to know if we were going to be together in the long term."

"Did he ever visit you in Hong Kong?" I asked.

"No. I went back home a lot to see him instead. I think that was part of the problem. When I decided to stay here and join the NET scheme, we broke up."

"So that was recent?"

"Yeah, it's frustrating because I really love him, but it isn't practical. I can't find work in Canada."

"I know how you feel," I said. "My long distance boyfriend and I thought we'd finally be together this year, but it still hasn't happened."

"How long have you guys been long distance?"

"We've dated for almost three years, but for two and a half of them we've lived in different countries."

Eyebrows rose all the way around the table.

"That sounds so hard! I don't think I'll be able to do it for that long," said Emma.

"I *know* I couldn't do it. I missed Eddie so much in the two weeks that I was here before he arrived," Sam said of her fiancé. "There's no way I could handle two years!"

"Hopefully I'll be able to move to London in a year," I said. "I guess it's always helped that there's been an end in sight; the end just keeps moving a little bit further away each time. We communicate really well…

and we know it's worth it." My excuses sounded hollow. I'd told people the positive aspects of long distance dating for so long that I didn't know whether I believed them myself anymore. We really did communicate well—that's all we could do. "So, anyway," I tried to change the subject, "Melanie, have you made friends with a lot of locals in Hong Kong?"

When we returned to the NET session, we heard that some teachers found it difficult to connect with anyone in their schools and experienced extreme isolation. Again, I wished they'd held the induction back in August. In some schools the local teachers, especially the local English teachers, resented the NET's presence. Sometimes NETs were also caught in the middle of power struggles, which might involve them being forced to attend a lot of Cantonese meetings or work Saturdays. Most schools, we were told, were very hierarchical, and not every principal was as friendly and reasonable as mine was. I had gotten lucky. I wondered again why the previous NET left my school.

One of the primary pieces of advice we got from the presenters was to build a support network outside of school. When our colleagues grew distant and our superiors rejected our ideas, we would want support. We needed people around us, families, friends, each other, to help our transition to the new environment. Sam glanced at me and Emma beside her, then scribbled her Facebook name onto two scraps of paper and handed them over. "Come to my birthday drinks! And my friend is having a junk boat party. You guys have to come."

"I'll be there," I said, writing down my phone number.

"I'm afraid of water," Emma whispered.

12

CANTO CLASS

I still wanted to be able to communicate with my co-workers. It took effort for them to speak English with me, and it seemed only fair for me to learn Cantonese. I signed up for a group Cantonese class at the YMCA in Tsim Sha Tsui, a notorious tourist hotspot on the Kowloon side of Victoria Harbour. The building itself was swanky for a Y and housed a kindergarten, rooms for various adult education classes, a pool, athletic facilities and a fully functioning hotel. The course I'd signed up for came widely recommended as the best cheap Cantonese class in town.

I showed up early the first day and joined a line outside the door. The hallway was decorated with signs of kindergarten life, and I could see little chairs and charts with weather words in the classrooms. The door was actually unlocked, but no one wanted to be the first one to enter the room. For nearly fifteen minutes, almost fifteen of us stood in a line in the cramped hallway outside an open room. Some people dug through their purses trying to make themselves look busy. Some people played on their cell phones or made awkward conversation with the strangers around them. Some people simply watched the others out of the corner of their eyes, shifting from foot to foot as they waited for someone else to lead. When the teacher finally arrived, right on time, it was like a spell had been broken and everyone tumbled through the door talking and laughing.

The teacher was a local Hong Kong woman named Cherry. She had one lazy eye, so when she called on you in class you could never tell if she was actually talking to you or the student to your left. She did not assign homework, and the lessons were very informal: the students got out of it what they put in.

We began the first lesson with the standard language class round of introductions: "Hello. My name is Cherry. What's your name?" or "*Neih hou. Ngoh haih Cherry Louhsi. Neih giu mutye-a?*" We fumbled through those first words, starting to recognize pieces of phrases we'd heard but hadn't understood before. By this time we had already figured out how to say our pleases and thank yous, contained in the single word: "*mhgoy*".

I learned how to say, "I am an English teacher."

"*Ngoh haih Shannon. Ngoh haih Yingman Louhsi.*"

Cantonese is a harsh language, and I equated it with German, the language I had studied in high school. There six nine tones, and we practiced saying identical syllables six different ways, each pronunciation communicating a separate meaning. It was hard to hear the difference between the rising and falling tones. I could distinguish the low, middle and high tones by ear, but when I tried to pronounce words in the high level tone, I ended up speaking louder instead of higher, "MA!" The class just laughed. Half of them were doing the same thing. I wished my ear for music and accents was better; it might have helped.

The class itself was friendly and fun, like a sociable meeting of the United Nations. There were representatives of all ages from Ireland, Panama, Hungary, Peru, France, India, the Philippines, England, the USA and even Cameroon. Most knew a few Cantonese words here and there, but not all were newcomers to Hong Kong. I spoke to a beautiful Indian woman named Kashaana who had lived in Hong Kong for five years without ever taking a language class. She didn't seem to know much more of the language than I did, but her young son was starting to learn it in school and she wanted to keep up with him.

There were two other NET teachers in the class, both tall, good-looking Irishmen. The first, Ian, made friends instantly, and before half the class was over he was joking with the teacher and trying out the phrases he'd picked up at his school on our classmates. He was one of those people who acquire languages like they're picking up groceries. The second Irishman, David, had been in Hong Kong for three years already. He had curly brown hair and deep smile lines around his eyes. He had never taken a Cantonese class, and his language abilities were probably closer to mine. Ian had dragged him to the class.

It was not so surprising that David and Kashaana had lived in Hong Kong for so long without learning any Cantonese. You don't need to speak it to get around in most areas of Hong Kong and it would be easy to live here forever and never learn a word of the dominant language. English lessons are compulsory all through school, so you are always able to find a local who remembers a few words. Even if their English is no better than that of the weakest teachers at my school, you can still order food and get help in shops. I heard about expats who had been in Hong Kong for eighteen years without learning to say anything in Cantonese except for their address to give to taxi drivers and a polite "*mhgoy*" (thank you).

My Cantonese knowledge improved at a glacial pace, and it was difficult to find people to practice with. I could only say the most basic phrases, and any time I tried to use my Cantonese words in a shop, people would speak English back to me to save time. I asked Ian how he was able to progress so quickly and get people to speak to him in Cantonese. "I just love languages," he said. "When I was living in Japan it was more important to speak the language. I don't want to waste the opportunity now that I'm here."

"Do you think you'll ever go back to Japan?"

"Actually, I'm hoping to find a local girl to marry and settle down in Hong Kong," he said.

"That's specific."

"I'm almost thirty-two. Besides, I like Chinese culture and the prospects are better here than back home in Ireland, that's for sure." The EU was shuddering in pain at this time, so I could understand his worries about the job prospects. However, his determination to find and marry a local girl was harder to grasp. So focused on one man and my hopes for a future with him, I couldn't understand how someone could just pick a spot and make it work with someone—anyone—there. What about the connection with one person that couldn't exist with anyone else, the feeling that they knew you better than everyone in the entire world? I had crossed oceans for Ben, uprooted my life and molded my plans so they would be in sync with his. Would I have done the same if I'd been like Ian, thirty-two and ready to create a relationship in whatever place seemed convenient?

David met my eyes when he looked up from a vocabulary list. I tried to imagine what would have happened if I'd come to Hong Kong single. I still would have met these two, would have spent two nights a week chatting during breaks, maybe going for a drink after class. Perhaps I would have been interested in trying an international relationship here, a city that was less romantic than London but had an electric, passionate energy. I'm sure I could make it work, and at least we'd get to see each other regularly.

Unbidden, scenes from the month after I arrived in Hong Kong played through my mind like a movie trailer. Ben, squeezing my shoulders as we rode through the night on the Airport Express, the city lights passing us like spaceships. Ben, speaking Cantonese to a man at the goldfish market, asking the price for a bag of iridescent blue fish, accepting the man's compliments on his pronunciation. Ben, waxing lyrical about the fancy kitchen goods store in Prince's Building. Every memory of those weeks was tied to him, his face inextricable from the market scenes and city lights surrounding it.

No, it wasn't enough for me to find a place in this world that I liked. I wanted that person whose passions were eclectic, bursting out like kernels of popcorn at unexpected moments. That person who engaged people, regardless of language, that expert conversationalist who always held a little of himself back. Ben had seen the way I was sometimes out of step socially, and teased and loved me for it. He saw the things I was good at, and had even more confidence in me than I had in myself. He had that peculiar brand of characteristics that made sense to no one more than me.

Yes, I could forge a romance with someone else, but I didn't want to.

It would be less than six months before my certainty was challenged to the core, before I'd wonder whether my twenty-two-year-old naivety shouldn't have paid attention to the practicality of Ian's plan.

13

NIGHT LIFE

It was my new Canadian friend Samantha's birthday, so we met up at a bar called Bourbon Street in SoHo (South of Hollywood Road) on a Saturday night. Like its sister neighborhoods in other cities, Hong Kong's SoHo had art galleries, restaurants and bars from around the world. There was a pub called the Yorkshire Pudding, an Italian wine bar, a French café, a Mediterranean taverna. It felt like Europe, and I lived just across the street, on the north side of Hollywood Road. Bourbon, which was near the end of Elgin Street, had tall, dark tables and murals of jazz musicians on the walls. They played classic rock and good country music, and I felt at home as soon as I walked in. Sam had picked it for her birthday drinks because they made a cocktail she liked called The Sweet Sensation. "Try this," she said, pushing the glass toward me as I sat down.

"That's very sweet." I puckered at the sugary concoction and ordered a ginger cocktail. Sam introduced her fiancé Eddie, a big, artsy guy who wore a fedora over his shaggy haircut. They'd brought along Eddie's friend Charlie, who had recently spent a month traveling around Mainland China. Charlie shifted in his seat and said, "Everything's too clean here. This isn't China."

"What part of China did you visit? I've always wanted to go to Shanghai," I said.

"I hated Shanghai."

"Oh… well, I've only been to Beijing before."

"Beijing was ugly and crowded," Charlie said. "I only wanted to go to the poor, unpopulated areas."

"Oh…" The conversation waned quickly, so Eddie and I talked about Chaucer for a while instead.

Sam, Eddie and Charlie had just been to visit the Big Buddha that day. It was the largest seated outdoor statue of Buddha in the world, located on Lantau Island. Ben and I had gone there when I visited him in Hong Kong the previous year. We had taken a cable car over misty island hills to get to it, and from up high we watched fishermen in the river below. The Buddha itself was less interesting.

"I didn't expect it to be so… touristy," Sam said. "I was kind of hoping it would be a spiritual experience and we could visit a monastery and escape for the day."

"I was expecting the same."

Eddie added, "The worst part is you get into the base of the statue that is this huge religious symbol—and there's a gift shop. The whole place is about commerce, not spirituality." I agreed; the statue was impressive, but not awe-inspiring.

"We went for the vegetarian lunch inside the base of the statue that was supposed to be served by monks, but it was just another noisy Chinese restaurant. Not that there's anything wrong with that, of course, but it's not what I was expecting," Sam told me as she stirred her Sweet Sensation.

"It was tacky," Charlie said bluntly.

Some of Sam's Canadian friends joined us, and they brought a round of Jaeger Bombs with them. I met Regina, a dead ringer for actress Amy Adams, and her elementary school friend Brittany. They had moved to Hong Kong together after Brittany's brother paved the way by joining the NET scheme. They introduced us to a revolving door of people who came and went between our party and various other engagements. We ordered more rounds as the lights dimmed in the bar and Sam's laughter went up an octave. "In Windsor, we used to go to the bar and drink like this every night during the year we were unemployed," Sam shrilled. "Not having a job sucked, but we had some great times!"

Despite living so close to the action, I hadn't really done the legendary Hong Kong nightlife properly yet. Sam's friends had been in Hong Kong for longer than the rest of us, and they knew their way around the bars, so off we went. I had never been the clubbing type, but the general good humor of the people around me coaxed me to relax and open up. We left Bourbon, moving from bar to bar. We picked up another friend of Regina's, a big Texan who took us to a bar down an alleyway right by my apartment building. "This place is the shit," he said. It was narrow, poorly lit, and loud. The volume of the music prohibited most conversation, so we sat around on low seats for a while, trying to look hip. I shifted around, trying to lean casually on the piled cushions. There weren't enough to be comfortable, but too many to use as a natural backrest. Abandoning my efforts to look cool, I sat forward and sipped my Corona, listening to Eddie shout over the music about backpacking in Australia. Soon, the Texan rounded everyone up and we moved on.

We traipsed the cobblestone streets and sidewalks between SoHo and Lan Kwai Fong (LKF). Groups of men in open-collared shirts and women in short, sequined dresses filled the spaces in front of each venue, their laughter filling the cool night air. The lights from the bars and buildings cast sharp, daylike shadows on the pavement. LKF is an L-shaped street in Central where bankers, lawyers and traveling businessmen go to party after work and tourists gather to witness. Sometimes they stay all night. The drinks are expensive; the people are glamorous; the bars are crowded. Living nearby, I could hear the sounds of partying all night, every night. On this evening, I was part of the hazy, surreal scene.

Around 1 a.m. we lost Charlie while on the way to a new place. I tried my first Jack and Coke—and liked it. Sam was laughing and talking about her upcoming wedding and how much she loved Eddie, Hong Kong and everyone around her at that moment. We stepped into a nightclub where no one was dancing.

By 2 a.m. I was feeling the lubricating effects of the alcohol. My fingertips tingled, and warmth and goodwill seemed to be multiplying in my stomach. I made plans to look at wedding dresses with Sam for her wedding. "You're going to love Ben, if he ever comes back!" I shouted over the music. Charlie reappeared and we tried out the Russian ice bar. I had been to one in London where the seats, walls, bar and glasses were all made of ice. This one was more like a walk-in freezer where you could take pictures in the cold. The walls weren't even made of real ice.

By 3 a.m. we found our way to a club in Lan Kwai Fong called Insomnia. It was crowded and everyone was on the dance floor. A live band played party classics from the 90s and 2000s. Sam and Eddie left to find Charlie, who had disappeared again, and I stayed behind with my new friends. I danced… I sang… I was having fun! It was hot, and my arms connected with sweaty backs and moist hands. The room spun around me. Squished in between a couple of Canadians and the big Texan and his girlfriend, all I could do was smile and try not to spill my beer. The band played songs I knew. I hadn't liked the crazy parties in college, but I was enjoying this. These people around me were all interesting and successful with fascinating conversation, though it occurred to me that I hadn't been able to hear anyone speak for the last hour. I cheered along with the crowd as the band played Blink 182.

I stumbled home at 4 a.m. leaving my new friends still going strong on the dance floor. My home was only two blocks from Insomnia. I could go there every night—if I was crazy. Feeling pretty good, I called Ben to say goodnight. He was happy to hear from me and amused at my befuddled state. We talked until dawn as the light came on again in the police compound. I wondered what the caretaker thought about the noise still coming from LKF. I wondered if she could even hear it through the fortifications of the facility.

I went to sleep with the early morning sun streaming through the window.

14

KOWLOON POETRY

For several months I'd been getting to know the neighborhood where my school was located. It was in Jordan Valley in eastern Kowloon, and as different as dragons and dandelions from the intoxicating international area where I lived. Each morning, I left behind one world and entered an entirely different, more Chinese one. It was the sort of place where restaurants didn't have English menus and people gave me funny looks for being a foreigner. Kowloon Bay was an up-and-coming area in the sense that it was still being built up, mostly with government housing projects for low-income families.

When I exited the MTR, which traveled above ground by the time it reached Kowloon Bay, I would join the crowd at the top of the escalator and make my way down into the station. A few people pushed and shoved, but when I cleared the bottleneck of the escalator most of the crowd peeled off toward a different exit. At my exit, I would swipe my Octopus card at the turnstile. The Octopus could be used to buy snacks and travel on the MTR, buses, trains and even ferries. My 30-minute commute cost just over a dollar.

Outside the MTR exit I'd stop by the St. Honore Bakery and Cake Shop for a barbecued pork bun, a popular local food that I had adopted enthusiastically. If the girls who worked there hadn't opened yet, I would pick up a less desirable packaged roll from the 7-Eleven. The man who worked at 7-Eleven usually looked distracted and sad. He disappeared after a few months and was replaced by a motherly lady who told me I was *hou lehng* (pretty) almost every morning.

I took a covered walkway from the station exit. A fresh breeze blew across the walkway, carrying the tiniest tinge of salt from the bay. It was always crowded in the morning. Mothers walked uniformed little children to school and older students trudged beneath backpacks by themselves. Young people made their way to work and older people, who weren't going anywhere in particular, lingered in the corridor. A very old woman often stood at the mouth of the walkway, making it more difficult for all of the commuters to squeeze through. She collected used newspapers from all the passers-by. I'd only ever seen three foreigners in this corridor, and there were never any on the final stretch before I reached the school. I used to think there were expats everywhere in Hong Kong, but that definitely wasn't the case.

Halfway along the walkway there was a bend and another bottleneck, where a free newspaper was given out each morning. The people shuffled together, hands reaching, elbows jabbing. Many of the elderly readers took their papers and immediately stood in the middle of the walkway to read and chat. For me, the walk to school was an exercise in agility. I had to dodge the little kids running for the school bus without bumping into the elderly or knocking over the stacks of newspapers. It was a lively place to be first thing in the morning.

I began to notice the regulars on my walk. I'd recognize a mother-daughter pair that held hands as they walked together, though the daughter was in her teens. There was a thin-faced teenage boy who looked like one of my own students. A whole collection of three-year-olds wore matching red backpacks and checkered uniforms as they toddled along each morning. Even though I never talked to them, recognizing these people made me feel at home in the neighborhood. Over the course of a few months, fewer people stared at me, or maybe I just didn't notice it anymore.

As I continued up the walkway, my school would come into view. There were two other schools directly across the MTR tracks from us, also housed in large new buildings. The area was growing rapidly, and new housing projects, each 30-40 stories tall, were taking shape on the ridge above my school. On the not-too-distant horizon stood countless apartment buildings. It was hard to fathom that each of the thousands of windows represented several people, and this was just what I could see from one spot on one of Kowloon's nine hills (technically eight real hills, each home to a *feng shui* dragon; the ninth dragon was, traditionally, the emperor). There were so many people packed onto this peninsula and collection of islands. It was hard to get my head around the numbers.

When I reached the end of the walkway, back on solid ground, I'd turn in the direction of some shops and the entrances to the local housing projects. The left fork led to my school, winding around a small park consisting of a concrete expanse, several benches and potted trees. A brick path hugged a steep slope on the way to the road above. The slope was covered in perma-freeze concrete, like nearly every other slope in Hong Kong. The local authorities used to spend hours cleaning up after landslides on the many Hong Kong hills and peaks. The solution was to cover every slope everywhere in concrete. It didn't matter if the slope was in a park or along a trail in one of Hong Kong's many areas of natural beauty: every slope needed a good strong coating. A sign with a registration number had been bolted onto each slope.

I remembered a story from one of my grandma's letters. In her days here, it was not unheard of for people to have yards and gardens. However, the old Hong Kong gardens could be dangerous places. In her letter dated 1959 my grandma wrote:

Earlier this year we had a bit of excitement in our neighborhood. It was during the rainy season and it had rained steadily for three days. Part of the hill which rises above our building all along one side

*gave way and came sliding down against our apartment. The weight
was so great that, besides filling in the driveway to the second floor
level, it pushed in the windows of the boys' room and the earth came
tumbling in! Fortunately, it happened during the day and the room
was empty so that no one was hurt. Nevertheless, for some time there
was much confusion which seemed to center about our household, as
the only entrance to the six apartments had suddenly become through
our garden and into and out of our house. Of course, Ayden and Bruce
[my dad and uncle] were thrilled with all the activity. Scores of coolies
with small reed baskets hanging from either end of bamboo "coolie-
bars" across their shoulders worked from early morning till nightfall
each day for one week just to clear away the dirt. Shovels and picks
were the only "modern equipment" used. Incidentally, many of the
coolies who did this heavy work were women. Our rooms had to be
cleared of mud and debris and repainted, and windows and frames
replaced. Only very recently has the hillside been put "in order" so that
everyone can rest more or less assured that the same thing won't happen
again. (1959)*

The paved slopes were less picturesque than a garden full of papaya and
bougainvillea, but at least they didn't go sliding into people's bedrooms.

Sometimes I saw people walking bent-backed up the concrete slopes,
spreading their laundry out to dry or sitting there in the sunshine. Others
did their morning exercises on the slope. I'd walk past the graying,
wrinkled men and women in pajama tops and soft shoes, raising their
arms to the sun in measured calisthenics. They swayed their hips in
slow circles like hula dancers, twisted their hands in careful Tai Chi, and
leaned on fences for balance as they lifted their feet into the air. There
was a meditative pace to their movements. You could tell that they would
continue to rise with the sun and do the same motions every morning for
the rest of their lives.

I usually arrived at work at the same time every morning, so I saw the same group of old people every day. Presumably, they were all residents of the housing projects above the park. I always wondered what they did for the rest of the day. In Hong Kong many elderly people live with their offspring and take care of their grandchildren. In the afternoon, lots of them were still in the park, with fresh faces added to the mix. In the afternoons they weren't exercising, but sitting on the benches or standing and chatting with the neighbors. Sometimes I would see someone mending socks or drying out small dead creatures on a screen in the afternoon sun.

The most memorable fixture in this elderly neighborhood gang was a tiny, wiry old man with a thick shock of gray hair who spent his mornings training with a spear. The spear was about as tall as him and was covered from the tasseled spearhead to the shepherd's crook end in spiraled silver ribbons. The head of a seahorse was carved onto the crooked end. The man's fluid movements spoke of a life of dedication to his art. Being on the older side of seventy didn't prevent him from spending the morning drilling the powerful forms. Another regular was a round, balding old man who took a walk each morning with a round, balding old dog. The dog always wore frilly pink frocks or t-shirts; its disgruntled pug nose sniffed along the ground as it followed the man.

By the time I crossed the road and reached the school gates, I would feel ready to begin my day, to step into the children's lives and see what difference I could make. My friend Choi Sze Hin came running up to me one day, holding the hand of little Anita from his class. "Miss Young! She is my friend!" he said, beaming. Anita smiled and waved and said, "How are you today?" They ran off across the playground, hand in hand. Every day after lunch when I spread English memory games across the picnic tables, Choi Sze Hin would come to play. He brought along a few more of his classmates each time. A girl named Molly spoke to me regularly, and she started bringing along her friend Angel. Anthony, who I met at the beginning of the year, always said hello too. Anson, another student, only came over to play games if there were prizes involved, but he loved to talk to me about the American pop stars he saw on TV.

I was becoming surprisingly popular with the students. They all smiled and waved when they saw me and called out my name. My smiling at the beginning of the year had paid off. The students impressed and charmed me. I learned a lot from them: obvious things, like how to write an effective lesson plan and how to set up my classroom better to avoid behavioral problems, but also about their lives. I learned more about their backgrounds, which students had siblings, and which ones had special needs and behavioral problems. Every day I remembered more of their 300 English names.

Once, I taught a short unit about rhyming words to my eight-year-old students. Their English was good enough that they could form their own sentences, so their teacher Miss Chan and I decided to challenge them creatively by asking them to write a four-line poem. We were both curious to see what they would produce. In class, we brainstormed rhyming words and wrote a few example poems on the board. The students listed all the words that they could think of that rhyme with cat (bat, fat, rat, mat, sat) and then I asked them to make a sentence that rhymed with "I have a cat." After some prompting, they rose to the challenge: "It is fat," "The cat's name is Matt," "I see a rat."

"Okay, now write four lines like this." A few picked up the thread right away. Jason wrote something like this:

She is Kate
She is eight
She lives in Kowloon
She looks at the moon

The very shy and bright Anna handed me a poem like this:
My name is Bunny

I am funny
And I eat honey
Because today is sunny

I was pleased to see the students completing the assignment with their limited English vocabulary, but there were a surprising number of directly duplicated poems. Copying was a chronic problem; I regularly caught students copying each other's answers on worksheets too. As long as the answers were right it did not seem to matter how they got them. Perhaps this was an effect of holding test scores and accuracy as the highest values in the system.

I was surprised that even some of my best students used each other's lines. Molly wrote:

I have a dog
And I have a frog
The dog is on the floor
And the frog is near the door

And her friend Angel wrote:

I have a dog
And I have a frog
The dog is on the floor
And the frog is near the door

As long as the rhyme was good, Angel saw no reason why she should not use it too. Still, I was encouraged by Steven's poem that defied the formulaic creativity of his classmates. He wrote:

I have a cat
It is fat
The cat has mouse
The mouse in house

The house's garden has trees
The trees has bees
The bees name was Ben
The house has a pen
A cat is happy
A mouse is funny

When I read this poem over his shoulder, I was excited—until I picked up Bobby's poem, which was written in the same formula. Now I didn't know who was responsible for the creative structure. Even so, it was exciting to see progress in my students, even as I noticed progress in myself. I was eager to improve my teaching and eager to understand the kids—and my colleagues—a little bit better.

15

JUNK TRIP

A group of Westerners in sundresses and board shorts stood amongst beach towels and duffel bags when I arrived at the pier. The sun reflected off aviator sunglasses and warmed bare shoulders. It was the first weekend in November, and Sam had invited me to go on a junk trip. Junks are boats that were once used primarily for fishing, but now people take them around to the islands for a day of swimming, drinking and general merry-making in the sunshine. There were a few familiar faces.

"Oh hey! I remember you guys from NET induction," I said. "Nova Scotia right?"

"Yeah. I'm Shane and this is my girl, Lauren. Man, this boat trip is gonna rock."

"I remember you." I joined Sam and her fiancé Eddie, who was slathering a thick layer of sunscreen over his tattoos. Sam told me Regina had been the one to organize the trip, but she hadn't arrived yet. We made a round of introductions as we waited for her. We were standing near the Star Ferry pier in Central, but when the whole group had assembled, a representative from the boat company whisked us onto a bus. We drove for half an hour to get to a different dock, in Sai Kung, where our boat was actually moored. Sai Kung was an idyllic beach town, with restaurants and village houses lining the main streets and boats lining the waterfront.

A burst of cool sea air met us as we stepped off the bus and walked to the end of the dock, flip-flops slapping the boards. I expected the junk to be a fanciful, oriental-looking creation with ribbed sails and lanterns hanging from the stern. I remembered my grandparents talking about their Chinese junk, which became an important part of their lives in Hong Kong. In the Christmas letter dated 1960, Grandma described it.

It is about 25 feet long and is equipped with a 15 horsepower outboard motor and two sails. We generally go to one of the many beaches on neighboring Lamma Island to picnic and spend the day. We've also enjoyed several evening outings when the moon was full and bright. I'm sure when the time comes for us to leave Hong Kong, parting with the Hai-ma (Chinese for seahorse) will be as difficult as parting with some of the dear friends we have made here. (1960)

Sadly, the sail-clad junk boats had disappeared from Victoria Harbour, apart from one that had been saved for tourists. The junk we were now boarding was a nice, polished teak boat with a modern motor and plenty of room for tables and cushioned benches. As soon as everyone was on board, the cool, young Chinese people working on the junk offered everyone beer and iced punch. We dumped our backpacks underneath the tables and explored the little vessel. There was a small cabin with a bathroom below deck and an open-air kitchen. The roof had rails and cushions piled on it so people could lounge in the sun, but there were no sails.

We pulled away from the dock and were soon speeding through the water. The famous Hong Kong skyline vanished behind us. Little islands appeared and disappeared on either side. The boat rocked in the wake of passing freighters and ferries. The weather was absolutely gorgeous, with no sign of clouds or pollution haze anywhere. I couldn't believe that this was early November. We heard the soft rush of water all around us. With a cool breeze in our faces and cold drinks in our hands, we'd suddenly been transported from a busy metropolis to the glossy pages of a tropical cruise brochure.

Most of the group gravitated to the roof. I climbed the cool metal ladder and joined them there, where we got to know each other as the ocean spray misted our faces. We alternated between sharing stories and staring in wonder at the sun and the sea all around. The people were mostly teachers (some NETs, some at international schools, some music teachers), and I discovered a diverse range of interests and backgrounds. One of the music teachers, Rosaline from Mexico, was also an opera singer. Kaela, a fellow American, had taught in five different countries by the age of 29. There was a pretty, blonde Australian journalist named Jayne, who told us about going to a fight night for investment bankers. James was an actor fresh off the boat from the UK who'd taken a liking to Regina when they met on a night out near LKF. A common denominator between us was that we'd all be facing extremely poor job prospects in our own countries if we'd stayed there. We felt lucky to be in Hong Kong and we were optimistic about our futures.

Shane told us, "I was subbing every single day for an entire school year in Canada. I worked more hours than the other teachers in the school and my income was still below the poverty line."

"There are just no jobs, and we're talking no jobs for the next ten years," added Lauren.

An American said, "My teacher friends back home haven't had a raise in three years. Their bonuses were $300 last year. It's insulting."

"We're definitely living the good life here now. Cheers!"

I noticed that many of the teachers who had arrived for one- or two-year contracts never found good reasons to leave. The lifestyle for an expatriate teacher was significantly better than a teacher could expect in a Western country. Teachers at home struggled with classes that were more crowd control than education, and too many of the students did not care about what they were learning. As the economy struggled, they were facing cuts to education budgets across the board, especially in my home state of Arizona.

On the other hand, Chinese culture demands a huge amount of respect for teachers, and the pay packages and low taxes in Hong Kong ensured that we all enjoyed a very high quality of life. I had looked at my bank account recently and realized that—despite the costs of relocating—I would soon have enough extra cash to pay off my smallest student loan early. Add that to the island location that boasted beach weather in November and lots of people got hooked on Hong Kong.

About half an hour after leaving the dock, our junk arrived off the shore of a beautiful white sand beach. The little cove was entirely cut off from the rest of the island and the only ways to get to the beach were to crowd into a little motorboat tied behind the junk or to hop into the water and swim.

I hadn't thought I'd be up for wearing my swimsuit around a bunch of strangers in November, but the water looked too inviting. The sparkling blue-green sea called to me in a voice full of refreshing promises. I changed in the tiny bathroom at the bottom of the boat and joined the group on the roof. The boat swayed as we climbed over the low wooden railing and clung to a foot-wide ledge on the other side. On the count of three my companions jumped off the roof into the crisp, blue water. After a panicked moment of hesitation, I plunged in after them, arms flailing.

A snapshot of the beach, the waves and the three swimmers in front of me imprinted itself on my eyes before the water hit me like a blast of air-conditioning in a Hong Kong shopping mall. It was perfectly cool and relatively clear. Once I had properly adjusted my bathing suit underwater, I emerged into the sunlight and glanced back at our boat. It looked quite quaint, with wood-paneled sides and the shaded party deck on top. The people left on the junk made their way down to the motorboat to take our supplies and towels to the beach.

After several months of sitting in the office and walking through smoggy, crowded streets everyday, the water was glorious. There was so much space, and I reveled in stretching out my arms and legs as I swam for shore. I reached the shallows of the little island and splashed my way onto the beach. The motorboat full of beer pulled up beside me.

On the beach we wiggled our toes in the sand and told more stories. There were no other people on the island apart from our group. A game of football started up in the sand. I joined a group of girls on a rocky outcrop at the edge of the beach and looked out at the sea. Alyssa was a teacher from upstate New York, near where I had gone to college. She had recently returned from taking her students on a school trip to Malaysia. "It's such a great opportunity to be here," she said, her subtle accent giving her words a familiar twist.

"Did you have any trouble meeting people when you first arrived?" I asked.

"Yes, definitely," she said. "People get caught up in their own thing, and in Hong Kong people come and go a lot. I was really lonely at first."

"What did you do to get connected with people?" I asked, thinking of my own lonely evenings.

"I met Catherine, who introduced me to *everyone*," Alyssa replied.

Catherine, a cheery teacher from England, laughed at that. "Isn't it lovely how you meet so many interesting people in Hong Kong?" she said, leaning back gingerly on the rock and turning her face to the sun. "I just love hearing everyone's stories." It was so cool to talk to a bunch of young women who were embracing their lives abroad. Before I left the US, numerous women (especially in their 40s) told me that they'd always wanted to live abroad. So many people said it was their dream, yet somehow their lives got in the way. They spent their 20s going to grad school, getting married and having babies (not necessarily in that order) and they had no space to breathe in between. By the time they hit 30 the babies and careers were there to stay. They felt they'd lost their chance to go out and experience the world. Not so with these women.

We chatted about our schools, our students and the places we still wanted to visit on our holidays. The sun beamed down from the clear November sky and cooked its way into our skin cells. Time didn't seem to exist here, and I wondered at the trail of circumstances that had brought me to this rocky perch in paradise. *I'll miss this if I join Ben in London next year...*

Even as the thought entered my mind, I sat upright. The sea glinted in the sun and laughter reached us from the makeshift football pitch. I concentrated on that thought, which had come so easily. *I'll miss this if I join Ben in London next year.* It was the first time I had used *if* instead of *when*. It had always been my plan to find work in London. I was saving money, and Ben and I really did need to spend time in the same country. But sitting on this rocky outcropping in a tropical paradise, the rainy streets of London seemed far away.

The call for food rang across the beach. We ran into the water for our swim back to the boat. Soon, we were hoisting ourselves up the cold stepladder and collecting towels, plates and meals. "Where's Regina? We shouldn't start without the birthday girl."

"She and James are making out on the island."

"Eh, let's dig in then." Greek salad, steak, potatoes, stuffed peppers and two different types of fish covered a countertop that rolled with the waves. The beer and punch continued to flow. When everyone had finished eating, someone brought out a rich chocolate cake to celebrate Regina's birthday.

The rest of the afternoon passed in pure bliss. We spread out on the cushions and napped in the sunshine. I chatted quietly with Rosaline, who had recently fallen madly in love with a German expat who split his time between Hong Kong and Australia. I recognized her "can't be without him for another three months" attitude as the one I had at the beginning of my relationship with Ben. Rosaline was getting ready to quit her job and follow her German to Australia. She was ten years older than me, but I felt like a sober long distance relationship veteran as I recommended that she have patience.

Just before sunset, everyone gravitated to the cushion-padded front of the boat, where we played games and admired each other's sunburns. Mine was the worst by far. The day before had been cold and gloomy, so I hadn't thought to put on sunscreen. It was November! Not even painfully reddening skin could ruin the moment though. As the sun dipped toward the horizon, we fell silent, watching the way it reflected through the quiet ripples marking our passage.

16

Storm Clouds

As November rolled on, a tropical storm in the Pacific Ocean developed into a major typhoon. Megi was rumored to be as strong as Hurricane Katrina, and people thought she would swing through Hong Kong. There was a signal system in place to warn against dangerous storms. A T8 signal meant that school and work would be canceled. The city would go into lockdown. I stocked up on food, water and snacks for typhoon day and prepared to watch the storm roll in from my big windows. If the wind got strong enough to shatter the windows and suck me out into the gale, I could spend the night with a blanket on my marble shower floor as the sub-tropical weather tore its way around my building.

I looked for storm clouds outside my window and checked on the weather preparations in the old police complex. I'd been noticing more activity there lately. The caretaker had appeared several times. She was in her late 50s and had close-cropped hair and round shoulders. She sometimes sat in a chair in the shade of the old barracks. Every once in a while people would walk across the courtyard inspecting the facility. One weekend an entire group of school children trooped through the grounds in their uniforms. I had done some research and learned that the city of Hong Kong was in the process of deciding how to develop the complex now that it was no longer being used by the police. Potential developers were required to maintain the structural integrity of the main buildings because of their historical significance. This was an unusual situation. Many of the traditional Chinese houses and old remnants of colonial Britain in Hong Kong had been torn down to make room for modern offices and apartments. Finally, they wanted to preserve this bit of history.

I loved the old building, and I felt conflicted about the coming changes. It would be fascinating to watch the old structures become something new. The original occupants of the complex must never have thought it could be used as anything but a prison and police station. However, the rate of change in Hong Kong was already so rapid that I wasn't sure I was ready for this.

I'd noticed there were always new businesses opening up around me. The rents had gone up on a street near my building, and almost every single shop on it was being gutted. A pizza joint had already replaced the smoothie bar on the ground floor of my own building, and a whiskey bar was moving in two floors above it. The Buddha Lounge continued to disgorge patrons into the morning light, but a dozen nearby restaurants were in constant flux. It was disconcerting to see everyone so optimistic about their economic prospects when my friends back home were in such precarious positions. Hearty conversations about business ideas, mergers, taxes and the stock market were common in Hong Kong. But the prosperity of the city was not without consequences.

Hong Kong was experiencing an unprecedented influx of people from Mainland China thanks to the nation's robust economic growth. The people I saw on Queen's Road, a popular shopping street, were not like the working-class parents of my students. These people from the Mainland, which now boasted a million millionaires (in USD), were eager to spend their newly acquired wealth. The tax conditions in Hong Kong made it cheaper to buy luxury items, which indicated a higher social status for the visitors. The Mainlanders would flood in with full wallets to buy designer clothes, watches that cost as much as my college education, and luxury cars. They were also buying property and driving up the prices for everyone else.

I regularly heard local Hong Kongers complain about the Mainlanders. They were used to being a separate entity from China, and tensions were rising. The Hong Kongers resented the competition and described the Mainlanders as loud and uncouth. Occasionally, someone would film a Mainland Chinese person allowing their child to defecate on the floor of a fancy shopping mall and the internet would light up with angry commentary on the situation.

The worries over China's rising power were not limited to different standards of etiquette. The local Hong Kong people also worried that their proud right to free speech was in danger since China had taken over the governance of the city. They enjoyed the prosperity brought on by Mainland money, but they were worried about the implications of being under the control of Beijing. It was an odd dynamic to witness. The British influence had poured into Hong Kong for over a hundred years, forever altering the culture of the island. Now an ambitious Chinese influence was pounding into the city and pushing back hard against the old colonial habits.

The changes in the city were energizing, but I worried about things spiraling out of control. The changes in Hong Kong made me feel off balance, although I suppose I'd been off balance since Ben flew away. I held onto the image of the old police complex, something that would have to adapt to the changing circumstances, but whose essence would remain. It was a necessary piece of stability as waves of uncertainty grew in my own mind. My uncertainty had little to do with economics.

As activity stirred in the courtyard of the old police station, storm preparations well underway, questions stirred in my mind. I used to know what I wanted to do with my life: work in book publishing, travel abroad, marry my best friend. My purpose was set, just like the primary function of that old building. But in Hong Kong I became less sure.

Living with so much change and independence around me was making me rethink what I actually wanted to do with my life.

In Hong Kong, I hadn't gotten involved in any of my usual activities, like fencing, public speaking groups, and church. Those things used to fill my time, overflowing and consuming my attention, but I didn't miss them. Instead, I was being introduced to a world of adventure, prosperity, the unexpected. Was this something that would have happened no matter where I ended up? Was I changing *because* of the city around me, like the old building? What if I changed even more? A few months in Hong Kong had shown me I was not yet the person I would be for the rest of my life.

Typhoon Megi decided to skip Hong Kong entirely and fly straight north to China. But another storm was brewing in my thoughts, one that frightened me worse than super typhoons and uncertainty over career choices. I'd always wanted to find the person that would be my best friend and partner for my entire life. When I met Ben, the pieces fell into place beautifully. He'd always challenged and encouraged me, and I'd been certain we would get along when we could finally be together. But what if it turned out that *he* wasn't what I wanted after all either? What if I used all this freedom and independence to explore other options? I was only 22! Most people would say that's too young to choose the person you want to be with for the rest of your life.

I was incredibly lucky: young, healthy, living and teaching abroad, making more money than I spent... But people kept saying to me:

"It's so great that you're making the most of your 20s experiencing the world."

"I had no idea what kind of person I would turn out to be in my 20s."

"I've changed so much just since I turned 18. I wonder what I'll be like when I'm 26."

"You have to know someone for at least five years before you really know them."

"You're only 22. You have plenty of time to figure out who you are."

It was not that I'd never heard these things before, but I hadn't really *listened* to what they were saying. I was 22 and sure of myself, after all. But as Hong Kong swirled, constantly changing around me, I started paying attention. I wanted to be with Ben. He said he wanted to be with me. We were being cautious, but my real fear was that I wouldn't want him anymore by the time we were finally able to be together. When I arrived in Hong Kong, I was fully prepared to stay for one year and then follow him to London next if he was offered a job there. Was that what I still wanted? What if I spent another year in Hong Kong regardless of where Ben got his next job? We already knew we could survive long distance…

And this was where panic waited, a subtext, a threat. I didn't want to become too comfortable being apart from Ben. What if we both got so used to the independence that we could stay apart for years? What kind of a relationship was that? The long distance time was just stretching and stretching and I was starting not to mind it.

17

FIGURINES AND INCENSE

December approached in a flurry of lights. My plane ticket was booked to visit Ben in London; I'd be spending Christmas away from home. I'd been looking forward to sending home a box of authentic Hong Kong trinkets for my big family. The most authentic trinkets would be cell phone charms from Japan and clothes tailored on the cheap in China, but I wanted to buy stuff that *looked* like it came from Hong Kong. So, on a sunny Saturday morning, I set out for the Cat Street antique markets.

Cat Street was a pedestrian lane lined with shops full of Buddhas, vases, wall hangings, statues of gods and goddesses, jade (both real and fake, although I couldn't tell the difference), and various good luck charms. In front of the shops were tables and stalls piled high with more affordable, non-antique versions of all of these things. Assorted souvenirs dedicated to Chairman Mao (watches and alarm clocks, little red books, statues, hats, and pens) lined the tables. I ran my fingers over the dusty objects and flipped through prints of beautiful Chinese women that appeared to be ads for cigarettes and airlines.

I still wasn't very good at haggling. Most of the stuff was not expensive, especially compared to souvenirs in Western Europe, so it didn't seem necessary to overdo the bargaining. The most effective strategy for me was indecisiveness. I spent so long choosing which cloisonné bracelets to buy for my sisters that the shopkeeper dropped the price just to get me to buy the things and go away.

I thought about my sisters as I shopped. The youngest was eight years old. The others were approaching junior high, wrapped up in high school, starting college. As I picked up little jewelry boxes and tried on bracelets for them, I imaged the changes they must be going through on the other side of the world as they figured out who they were.

Foremost in my mind was a surprising email I'd just received from Chelsea entitled "Wedding Plans". She'd sent it to our mom, her best friend and me.

So I've been thinking about the wedding a lot for a while now and finally talked to Francois about it today to tell him what I was thinking. I thought I'd type up a little list to bring you guys up to speed and get your thoughts.

I'm thinking about something of a sunset-color, beach, travel themed wedding. I don't want to hit people over the head with that, just have it be subtle. Especially since we don't actually live near the beach. And not the light blue/tan/seashell/anchor rope type thing. A classy, evening beach look. Colors would be something like pink, orange, yellow, and red. Maybe with some midnight blue occasionally. We can decorate a little bit with polaroid pictures of beaches (many that Francois and I will take while in South Africa).

I would love for it to be held outside or semi-outside. I want the reception and the wedding to happen in the same place, no figuring out cars to drive between places. I'm thinking perhaps a park or house-type hall with a large yard. Obviously, I'll want something inexpensive.

I'm hoping this will be a mid-afternoon event and won't require a full meal. Something small and light like little sandwiches, vegetable platters, hummus, falafel, etc...

The letter went on to describe more ideas for Chelsea's wedding in the US. This was a surprise because no one had yet heard that she and Francois were engaged. Back in Korea, she'd told me they wanted to get married, but they weren't sure of the timing. Now, they'd decided to do it as soon as their contracts in Korea ended. They wrote that they didn't know where they wanted to live or where they'd be able to find jobs, but they knew they would be together. Just like my grandparents.

Over the next few days we had exchanged a flurry of emails full of plans and schemes for getting Chelsea a wedding dress by April. They were going to come to Hong Kong to spend a week with me before meeting Francois's family in South Africa and then flying to the US. They didn't plan to apply for new jobs until after the wedding, and they didn't even know what country they'd live in next.

Chelsea decided she would get her dress in Hong Kong, where she'd have a better chance of finding one that would fit her tall Western frame than in the less-Westernized cities of Korea.

I made arrangements to fly home during my Easter holiday for the wedding.

It was all happening very quickly.

As I flipped through another pile of old prints in Cat Street, I thought about how differently we were handling our international relationships. What they were doing didn't seem logical to me: I always planned ahead. They'd been together for a lot less time than Ben and I had, but they didn't want to be apart, so they were getting married, never mind the uncertainty about jobs.

A voice in the back of my head said, "Why didn't *we* just get married so we could be together this year? Why am I *still* in Hong Kong when Ben's in London?"

Of course the rational bit of my mind responded, "But you two are getting to grow as individuals during your time apart."

"But we've been growing as individuals for the last three years? Isn't that enough?"

"You and Ben are still younger than Chelsea and Francois."

"We're not that much younger."

"Ben is waiting until he is sure he will have a job next year. Isn't that wiser in this economic climate?"

"But Ben is going to have a job next year, I'm sure of it. And Francois and Chelsea will find jobs, too. It's not like they (or we) are supporting a kid. If we can support ourselves then we could support each other."

"But you're not really ready. You would regret getting married too early."

"You're only saying that because that's what everyone else says."

"They have a point…"

I tried to put these thoughts aside as a ping-pong game of wedding suggestions began between my sisters, my mom and me. I was excited for Chelsea and Francois, but I worried they would regret their hastiness. Nevertheless, the thought remained at the back of my mind, like a remnant of incense, that maybe Ben and I should have done something like this too. At least then we'd be together. It had been three months since Ben left, and I could barely summon the feeling of his hand in mine anymore.

In a small alley off of Cat Street, I found a box full of little knobby carvings of minor deities. The men and women in the box rose from little stumps and retained the rough, natural look of the wood. I thought they were beautiful. The woman working behind the dusty shop counter helped me decide which little old man and which woman with flowing hair to buy for my parents. They only cost 30 HKD (4 USD).

Outside another shop, several trays full of exquisite carvings of animals and gods sat on a table in the shade. I picked up the little white figures, examining each one, imagining choosing one for each member of my family, carefully wrapping them up in soft paper and sending them home.

Just when I was working up the nerve to ask the woman in the shop how much they were in my rough Cantonese (*gei do chin-a?*), she spoke to me in excellent English.

"Can I help you find anything in particular?"

"I'm just looking for now. How much are these carvings?" I held up a little dragon.

"Well, these white ones are made of hippopotamus tusks. We carve them here in our shop and they are very beautiful. The cost is 350 dollars for the smallest ones. The ones in this tray are carved from mammoth tusks and they are double the price." She must have seen me recoil and back away because she quickly directed me to a third tray. "These ones are made from a dark cherry wood and are exactly the same except for the material."

"How much are they?"

"They're 80 dollars each." That was more like it.

She explained the significance of the different figurines as I dithered over which ones to purchase. All the animals of the Chinese zodiac were there (I was born in the Year of the Dragon), and there were many little statues of minor deities and the Buddha in various forms. I selected a delicate image of the Goddess of Mercy for my grandma and a little old man with a turtle on his shoulder for my grandpa. The woman explained that he represented long life and good health. My grandpa was 86 and one of the healthiest people I knew, so it seemed appropriate. I hoped the statues would be tiny reminders of my grandparents' many happy years in Hong Kong.

Finally, I made my way home with a handbag full of bracelets, wooden combs, a little clock, two small jewelry boxes, various lucky charms, and the carvings for my parents and grandparents. I laid out my purchases on the table and discovered I was short a gift or two. The Temple Street night market in Kowloon beckoned, and I took the MTR there after dinner to finish my Christmas shopping.

When I arrived, the sun had set and the market had already sprung to life. The Temple Street market was part of several different markets that stretched from near the Yau Ma Tei MTR station, around a huge old gated temple and all the way to Mong Kok, where it blended into the Ladies Market. At the Yau Ma Tei end, it sold fruits and vegetables, but soon morphed to include stall upon stall of tourist junk, watches, electronics, antiques and even sex toys. People sat at tables outside the local restaurants on the Yau Ma Tei side and ate hairy crabs and drank Tsingtao beer under the obscured stars.

After wading through the tables and looking enviously at the piles of seafood, I walked straight through the heart of the market. Antiques and fakes waited beneath the banyan trees. European backpackers, Indian tourists and teenage locals milled around the tables and bargained for goods. The shopkeepers shouted across the aisles to each other in loud Cantonese. I wished I could send pieces of the atmosphere home as gifts instead of the little bracelets of painted porcelain.

Where the Temple Street portion of the market met the Mong Kok portion, a side street branched off and wound around the back of the temple. A row of fortune tellers, palm readers, face readers and other types of sages stretched into the shadows beneath the temple walls. I wandered down the corridor as the fortune tellers grinned and beckoned for me to sit on the rickety chairs and stools in front of their stations. They were not the wrinkly and toothless soothsayers of stories; many were middle-aged or younger and they looked rather professional, apart from their dingy surroundings.

I'd never had my palm read before. In a "when in Rome" moment, I almost sat down at one of the booths. I'd heard enough stories about people who had their fortunes told with uncanny accuracy to be apprehensive about trying it. My future was full of uncertainty as I waited to see where Ben's life and mine would take us next. Those Temple Street sages might tell me something about the future that I wouldn't like. I lost my nerve. I didn't want to know what was going to happen. Besides, it was dark and most of the little booths were creepy anyway.

Further down the lane, I encountered three enclosed spaces, like the outdoor seating area of a grungy café without the café. They were in a row opposite the fortune tellers and each one contained several round tables with an assortment of plastic chairs and seated patrons. In each space a woman belted out a Cantonese opera ballad on a portable microphone. The speakers were large enough that I could hear each singer entertaining her audience from the street, all singing different tunes. The women competed for airspace as the music filled the brisk night. The one who seemed to be winning had a disgruntled musician accompanying her on some sort of stringed instrument; they looked like gypsies.

A few steps more and I started to smell something more potent than the usual incense. I felt a sense of foreboding along with the scent. Whatever the contemporary equivalent of the old opium habit was in Hong Kong, I didn't think this was a good time to find out. Perhaps I shouldn't be wandering too far down a dark street in a strange city when I was all alone. I headed back toward the lights of the shops on Temple Street. On my way back the fortune tellers started calling to me and I picked up my pace.

I dove back into the market, losing myself in the spirited commercial activity and the scent of new leather, seafood and incense.

18

MYSTERY

The activity at the old police complex beneath my window became more purposeful. One evening, the doors on the second floor of the barracks building were open, light pouring out across the balustrade. The outer doors of the police headquarters remained barred, but the gates to the courtyard had been flung open too. I discovered that a local foundation was holding an arts event, using the old buildings as a showcase for modern design and photography. I watched my private building as tourists and arts aficionados flooded through it. For several days I couldn't bring myself to actually go down the escalator and cross the road to it. Just as I didn't want to know my fortune, I didn't want the mystery of the old police compound to end.

I read an article announcing that the old police station would be renovated into an arts center after the current exhibit closed. This was the last chance anyone would have to explore the complex in all its derelict glory. Finally, curiosity got the better of me. I took a breath and left my apartment just an hour before the gates closed for the night.

Banners for the design festival waved in the gloaming from the lampposts on Hollywood Road. I crossed the street and entered the complex. Groups of people and photographers came in and out of the gates, but as I passed under the bright spotlight at the entrance, the light glared into my eyes and obliterated the world for a moment. This was how a prisoner must have felt when they entered these doors too, not able to see what would come next. Trepidation gripped me.

I climbed the steep path to the courtyard and took my first look at the massive headquarters building from the other side. The back of the building was decorated with ornate red and white brick and tile, an unexpected change from the dull gray front. Light tumbled out of the windows and doors. An elegant woman in a floor-length black evening gown was being photographed in front of the building, along with a tall man in a white tuxedo jacket. They looked like they had stepped out of a dinner party in the 1870s.

I entered the building. Patterned tile and dust covered the floor; peeling plaster cloaked the walls and columns. The windows were still boarded up. I wandered, and found myself alone in a little gallery. Black and white stands held pictures of Hong Kong in the 1800s. In those early colonial days, Hong Kong had been a jumbled, dusty city where the colonizers were carried around in sedan chairs and the locals wore brocaded silks or simple pajama-like suits.

As I wandered, a nervous excitement played through the pit of my stomach and up into my heart. I had a personal investment in these buildings. I'd been looking down at them every day and imagining romance and an exotic past. Now, I was actually exploring the nooks and crannies, peeking through the barred corridors and stairwells. It was a moment I had anticipated, but had never quite believed would happen. It reminded me of the first time I picked Ben up from the airport after our first three months apart. We didn't know what it would be like to be together again. We weren't sure if we would still get along. We were nervous that we would not be able to live up to each other's expectations. I remembered the exhilaration when we were finally together then, wrapped in a blanket of New York snow. I was in the same situation now: waiting, hoping, observing him on Skype like I had been observing this building. What would it be like when Ben and I finally got to live in the same city? Would we be surprised and enchanted by each other—like I was feeling now?

While exiting one gallery and wandering back down the main hall, I accidentally walked right in front of the elegant model in the black gown. The photographer and the tuxedo-wearing man were outside the window. It was like passing in front of the ghosts of another time: a wealthy local debutante on a rendezvous with a British officer.

I found my way out of the headquarters and walked across the courtyard to the barracks building. Many of the rooms were empty, with only bare walls and dusty light fixtures. Occasionally a mantle and blocked fireplace interrupted the monotony of the walls. Sometimes someone would walk out of a room I thought empty, and I'd jump before steeling myself to enter.

I imagined the building filled with life. Notices still hung on the walls for the police officers who used to work here, listing postings and timetable information. I peeked into the old mailroom full of empty shelves and faded labels. A steel desk sat outside one of the doorways and a pile of rubbish inside another. Signs warned the long-vanished officers to register all visitors with the main office and directed them to the mess hall and fitness rooms. I wondered what it was like in the early days, when the head officers would have been Englishmen stationed there to deal with any tension in the subjugated island, overseeing local police forces.

When I came to the part of the building that had modern art displays, it was jarring. These rooms were well lit, with modern printed material and a higher concentration of people. There was an eerie, hushed attitude to the visitors. They were as impressed by the building as I was. One room had black curtains covering all the walls, creating a backdrop for white paper and wire sculptures hanging from the ceiling. As I walked into the room, the Hong Kong street noise outside vanished completely. The only other person in the room did not make a sound either as she drifted among the sculptures.

I grew braver as I wandered through the building's core, climbing dimly lit stairwells and peeking into empty rooms. A concrete bridge took me straight into the red brick prison. Barbed wire lined the outside and heavy iron doors stood open everywhere in the corridors. The cells contained simple bunk beds, messages carved on the walls in Chinese characters, broken plaster. I coughed in the dusty, moldy spaces. I felt alone, even though I passed others in the narrow halls. At the top of a staircase strewn with plaster, I got a glimpse of the model couple above me. I went back down so as not to interrupt them.

Finally, I pushed through a particularly heavy set of doors back into the courtyard. The crisp air welcomed me back. On my way out, I passed a window and froze: I was looking straight into the caretaker's quarters. She was younger than I had thought, sitting at a small table by the door and eating from a tin plate. A ginger cat was licking crumbs off the floor in front of her. There was a desk with two fans and an electric kettle further back in the room. A calendar with pictures of Hong Kong hung on the wall. I met the caretaker's eyes for a brief moment.

Turning from the caretaker's kitchen, I looked up and saw my own building rising above the police headquarters. It was tall and narrow and surrounded by several shorter buildings, making it look like a raised thumb. The rusty pink bricks looked dull in the glare of the city lights. I could see my own dark window between the lighted ones above and below it. The last few visitors were making their way down the slope and out of the complex. I paused for a moment, watching my building and the scene below it. Even though I had now seen what those buildings were like, they hadn't lost their mystery after all.

19

CHRISTMAS DUMPLINGS

It had been warm in the beginning of December, but the weather finally turned. I started wearing sweaters for the first time and looked forward to unpacking my winter coat for Christmas in London. The Hong Kongers, used to the climate, had been wearing jackets and scarves for weeks. All of the businesses around me had decorated for Christmas. Lights and fake Christmas trees multiplied across the city. Displays of snowy villages, Santa's grottoes and festive Christmas trains appeared in the malls. People loved taking pictures of the displays, and for once it was not only the tourists who stopped to pull out their cameras and block normal pedestrian traffic. Every time I walked through the shopping malls and central squares, I saw locals posing with their kids in front of shiny plastic baubles and wrapped presents the size of cows.

The most striking sight at Christmas time was of the big skyscrapers in Central. The view was always arresting thanks to the lights from countless apartments and office windows, but at this time of year there was an extra splash of color on the skyscrapers. Season's greetings covered the buildings, broadcasting their messages across the sky like fluorescent Christmas cards. The words were in English. The Christmas carols playing in the shops invariably made me think of holidays at home. It could have been really depressing, but the lights brightened things up, and I didn't feel lonely. In fact, I felt rather optimistic. The city glowed around me.

Then, in the days before Christmas Break, London got hit with its worst snowstorm in thirty years. Heathrow Airport was shut for days as workers cleared out the crush of snow and people tried to get home. I watched the weather reports and flight statuses anxiously as the day of my departure approached. My friend Catherine from the junk trip had her flight home to England canceled. A sense of foreboding threatened the festive atmosphere. It had been over three months since I had last seen Ben. I didn't think I could take another delay. If I had to, I'd park myself in the airport and beg for the planes to fly to England.

On the final day of school, there were Christmas parties in each of the classrooms. In between anxious moments checking the weather conditions abroad, I went around to each of my twelve groups to say Merry Christmas. The kids gathered around me like baby birds and filled my hands with treats. They loved to share food. I couldn't bear to say no as little Anita and Choi Sze Hin stuffed packets of dried seaweed into my pockets.

That night, the school hosted a benediction ceremony to celebrate the first year it had spent in its new building. Visiting dignitaries were invited, including people from the Education Bureau, the bishop of Hong Kong and the principals of other schools. The only people who weren't invited were the parents and students of the school. My primary duty was to stand at the entrance looking like an American and bidding the visitors good afternoon. I had realized by now that a big part of my job was to be visible so everyone would know that our kids learned English from someone who looked like a bona fide English speaker. After the ceremony was over, the staff and a selection of the attendees bundled into a bus to go to a Chinese restaurant for a celebratory feast.

All the teachers and guests found seats in covered chairs around huge round tables. There was an obvious divide between the teachers and the visitors, who were there to schmooze with our principal. I was ushered into a seat next to June, who kindly insisted on being my host for the evening. We sipped tea and talked as the latecomers made their way into the remaining seats. I tried out a few of my Cantonese phrases. "*Ngoh haih Yingman Louhsi. Ngoh haih Mei-gwok-yahn. Ni-go haih chah.*" "I am an English teacher. I am an American (literally "beautiful country person"). This is tea." My co-workers laughed.

The teachers with weaker English skills, who usually didn't talk to me, shared their own phrases, remembered from school: "I like eat fish. I am Chinese. I live in Kowloon."

I smiled a lot and did my best to answer: "*Ngoh jung-yi sik chasiubao.*" "I like to eat barbecued pork buns."

The waiters came around offering drinks, like they would in any Western restaurant. Unlike at a Western Christmas dinner however, all the teachers declined the beer that was being offered and opted for soft drinks. I ordered a coke, which pleased the teachers: "You like Coca-Cola! You are American!"

The food was all preordered, and it came out dish by dish. The aroma of garlic and ginger and frying oil swept across the room with the arrival of each course. The tables featured large glass lazy susans to facilitate the family-style dining. It reminded me of my own family table. We had abandoned a typical rectangular dining table for a round table with a lazy susan long ago. It is much easier to squeeze extra siblings and their friends around a round table. Our lazy susan would be crammed with every dish at once, however. When I was a kid, we were under strict instructions to make sure no one was helping themselves to food before turning the disc (at the risk of spilling spaghetti or applesauce across the table and incurring Mom's wrath).

After we finished each dish of steamed vegetables or pork strips or dumplings, another assortment of steamers and platters containing an emperor's portion of Cantonese cuisine would appear. My favorite was the bamboo steamer of soup-filled dumplings or *xiao long bao*. They were little dough water balloons that you had to be careful not to puncture as you picked them up. The dumplings had savory morsels of meat and vegetables inside.

Unlike in my family, where it was first-come-first-served, my co-workers served each other whenever someone's bowl emptied. You had to pay close attention to whether your neighbor was getting enough to eat, cultivating a palpable sense of community. At times, though, I would grow impatient. Should I wait for the other person to serve me, when I really, really wanted one of those dumplings that had just been set down? Is it my turn to serve them? Am I even allowed to serve them? Finally, I grabbed a dumpling for myself. As I bit down, the liquid filled my mouth in a rush of flavor—and scalded my entire tongue. Tears filled my eyes as I set down my chopsticks. That's why everyone was waiting. *Xiao long bao* was fun to eat as long as you waited for the soup inside to cool.

June explained each dish to me if its identity was in doubt. I upheld my reputation by deftly handling my chopsticks throughout the meal, eliciting cheers from one or two of the teachers who hadn't seen this trick yet. My tablemates prompted the people sitting next to me to make sure that I tried each and every dish.

"Miss Young, have you eaten this?"

"Make sure Miss Young has some chicken."

"Miss Young, have some mushrooms. Very good! Very good!"

It pleased my companions whenever I particularly enjoyed a dish.

"Miss Young likes Chinese food! Very good! Very good!"

After we'd had enough rounds of meat and vegetables and dumplings to make me begin to think about being full, the kitchen produced a stomach-sized steamed fish. June gave me the cheek, which is the tenderest part. This was followed by one more dish of slimy vegetables, a plate of *chasiubao* (my favorite barbecued pork buns), and then a whole roast chicken. When I say whole I do mean whole. The head was included on the plate to reassure the diner that they were not actually eating a rat—which looks remarkably similar to a bird when roasted (or so I'm told). A huge bowl of noodles and a bowl of fried rice materialized after that.

Finally the waiters whisked away the remaining plates from the lazy susan. With practiced hands they spread clean bowls and spoons around the table and returned with a bowl big enough to cover most of the glass circle before us. It contained a gelatinous liquid swimming with curls and slivers of some sort of light brown something. Several teachers clapped their hands and everyone reached for the bowls.

"Shark's fin soup," June informed me. "Are you an environmentalist?"

What to do? Shark's fin soup is increasingly deplored because its key ingredient (the fin) is obtained in a gruesome manner. Fishermen catch the sharks, slice off their top fin, and toss them back into the sea. The sharks don't survive, and the rest of their bodies are wasted. Shark's fin fetches a high price, and the soup was popular, meaning that this practice was decimating the world's shark population.

However, I also knew that shark's fin soup was a traditional luxury served at Chinese weddings and special occasions. Hosts included it on the menu as a demonstration of generosity and prosperity. It was immediately apparent that my colleagues loved it. Should I make some sort of stand about the dish? Would that be an arbitrary judgment, given that I don't have moral objections to eating other meats? Would it be worth damaging the communal atmosphere at the table, when everyone was being so kind to me? I accepted the soup, but resolved never to order it myself.

At this point I was full to my ears and had lost count of the order in which the dishes appeared. Finally the wait staff produced yet another round of bowls and started dishing out a hot, sweet red bean soup. Hot bean soup as a dessert was a new concept for me, but fortunately some gelatinous rice and sesame confections appeared at the same time. Finally we heaved a collective sigh as the waiters quit bringing out dishes and a pair of young teachers bounced to the microphone. For a dreaded instant, I thought they were going to begin a round of karaoke. Instead, they began drawing names out of a box. "It's time for the lucky draw," June said. We had entered our names earlier in the meal, sometime between the shrimp dumplings and the plate of bak choy. A side table in the restaurant had been filled with wrapped gifts, mostly of the school supply variety, but there were also a few kitchen implements, food items and gift certificates.

The teachers chanted their friends' names. "Ka Man! Ka Man! Sze To! Sze To!" As each teacher or guest's name was called, the whole group cheered. I was next: "Miss Young!" The applause sounded louder than usual, warming my ears. My prize was a Wellcome gift certificate and an extra large pack of magnets, which I traded with June for some ginseng. Ironically, the ginseng had a big sticker on it that said, "Made in America."

At the end of the night there were many exchanges of "*sing daan fai lohk*" (Merry Christmas) and I walked to the MTR in the company of a few of my English co-teachers. For perhaps the first time I felt like one of the staff, rather than just the extra person that people had to look after. That is until one of the teachers started telling me how to use my Octopus card to ride the MTR. "Thanks, I actually take the MTR every day," I said. Her eyes widened in surprise.

20

LONDON FOG

The morning of my departure dawned. My flight was scheduled to leave on time, despite the continuing turmoil at Heathrow. I made it through security and immigration at Hong Kong International Airport with plenty of time to grab a gingerbread latte. *Just let the snow hold off for a little bit longer.* I kept my fingers crossed as I waited by the arrival gate, praying that there would be no bad news from England. I wouldn't mind getting stuck in London for a few extra days, but I couldn't miss this flight out of Hong Kong. My body remained stiff with tension until the plane was screeching down the runway.

Thirteen hours later I was dragging my suitcase and myself through the arrivals gate at Heathrow. I exited the bleak corridor inside the terminal and searched for Ben's smiling face and hazel eyes. He stood at the edge of the throng, a drop of oil on the surface of water, looking better than ever. My worries and loneliness melted like sounds in a crowd. Ben held me close, not speaking, and I pressed my face into the side of his neck, breathing in the precious scent of his shaving cream.

The airport was packed with travelers who had been stranded by the snow. Relatives milled about, waiting for their family members to walk through the doors. It was like the opening scene in the movie *Love Actually.* But I barely noticed them as Ben and I strolled through the terminal. "I can't believe I'm finally here," I said.

"We get almost two weeks together. Isn't it crazy?" he said as he squeezed my waist.

We barely had time to transport my suitcase to his apartment before we had to leave for his department's Christmas gathering. We traipsed across the cobblestones, shivering in the wind, and stepped into a warm diner. He worked in a swanky City office, but they had decided to hold their party at a greasy spoon for a laugh. The smell of frying fish and chips greeted us. I met Ben's boss and various co-workers and their plus-ones. Ben stayed close the whole time, his hand in mine. Leaning against his shoulder, it occurred to me that this is what it would be like to live in the same country as Ben the whole time. I would actually meet the people he told me about on the phone; he would know all of my friends. I felt glamorous telling people, "I just flew in from Hong Kong this afternoon," but imagined how nice it would feel to be a permanent fixture in his life—not just a long distance girlfriend.

For the next few days we cooked, ate, slept and took rambling walks through the frozen London streets and parks. We stamped through the rare city snow like we had the first time he visited me at college in New York. We returned to our old haunts, paid homage to the British Museum, wandered through the crowded shops on Oxford Street. We reminisced about the time we had spent together as students. A lot of things had changed since then, but our chemistry was not one of them. We laughed about how we didn't talk about anything but fencing for the first month, remembered that awkward Chinatown date that nearly made us give up on each other, visited the SoHo street corner across from a popular gay bar where we shared our first kiss.

After Boxing Day, we rented a car and set off on a road trip to Wales for three days. We had taken road trips in the US that remained some of our very best shared memories. Our first one had been punctuated by gasps from me anytime Ben's road decisions seemed risky. He hadn't had his license for very long, but he still sped confidently around tight bends through the Redwood Forest, the roads slick with rain. I'd spent that whole drive grabbing his arm and then apologizing for distracting him. I'd calmed down considerably in the last few years, trusting him more.

The Welsh road trip began at the London City Airport in a little VW Polo with manual transmission. I couldn't drive a stick shift, but in the UK it was too expensive to get a rental car with automatic transmission. All of the driving duty fell to Ben this time. He gripped the wheel, swearing and tensing as he operated the unfamiliar vehicle. The streets were still icy. As we maneuvered slowly out of the parking lot, I tried to be helpful without being distracting. "Are you doing okay?"

"Yeah, no wait, damn it. What's that car doing?"

"You're okay on this side."

"Are you sure?"

"Yeah, you have tons of space."

"I'll wait for the next opening." Sweat formed on his brow.

"I think you need to at least go the speed limit," I said carefully.

"This is fast enough."

"Seriously, everyone's passing you."

"I'm Chinese. It's in my nature to drive slowly," he snapped.

"You don't want anyone to run into you, so maybe just speed up when you feel comfortable."

"Oh shit." We stalled in a roundabout and he had to restart the engine. "The gears feel strange. We should have gotten the more expensive car."

"You'll get the hang of it. Okay, there's a light coming up." We stalled twice more on our way through the center of London. The walls of historic buildings rose around us. I tried to take pictures of passing statues without impeding Ben's view of the surrounding traffic. We made it to the M4 and headed west. I sat back and tried to relax.

As we drove through the English countryside and into Wales, the hills seemed impossibly green. Little stone cottages peeked above hedgerows along our route. It was a refreshing change from the concrete Hong Kong skyline.

We quickly discovered how strange the Welsh language looks to the unpracticed eye. We did our best to pronounce the words. "What does that sign say? Nawr Arafwych?"

"Wurfl mawr?" he replied.

"Myrnl wpudnurld?" I answered.

"Gwasanaethau!" We said it at the same time. That was the word for service stops along the highway and it ended up being our favorite. We took to shouting it at random moments throughout the trip ("Gwasanaethau!"). I quickly learned the phrase for slow down and used it frequently as Ben's confidence with the car increased. We turned on the radio and listened to Welsh football commentary (we think) as we approached our first destination: Cardiff.

We drove into Cardiff in the late afternoon, just after the castle had closed for the evening. In retrospect, late December was probably not the best time to travel around Great Britain. It got dark by 4 p.m. and the country was covered in a thick layer of fog. Because we couldn't go inside, we walked through the rainy streets illuminated by streetlamps and cheery leftover Christmas lights. Everyone in Wales seemed to be inside the pubs. By the time we made it to our bed and breakfast, it was completely dark and the fog had gone from an ethereal haze to a dense cream of mushroom soup. I was very glad I wasn't driving. When Ben safely delivered us to the door of our little cottage, we decided we were even for the time I drove us all the way from Niagara Falls to my college in Central New York during a blizzard.

We ate sumptuous Welsh food and drove around the countryside for the next few days. There were so many different ways to cook lamb! The Welsh countryside reminded me of Oregon, where my grandparents lived. It was so green and idyllic and organic that it was a shock to my system. We visited ruined castles, preserved castles, the ruined Tintern Abbey (of William Wordsworth fame), and a preserved coalmine, complete with a well-preserved miner/tour guide. As we explored, Ben would wrap his arm around my waist and say, "Don't leave!"

"Okay," I'd answer, not wanting to go anywhere. We explored little villages and listened to trilling Welsh accents. We got lost amongst the hedgerows and country lanes and wandered cold and windy beaches. We'd huddle in the car together with the heater blowing and I'd say, "Come back to Hong Kong with me."

"Okay," he'd answer. It was nice to pretend, even for a short time, that it could always be like this.

By the time we returned to London, I'd breathed in plenty of unpolluted air from the countryside and sea. We both felt refreshed, but the trip made us less willing to part than ever. Back in London, we spent our last few evenings doing the same thing: Ben would sit on the couch, reading bits of the newspaper or looking at his phone. I'd sit beside him, my head or my feet on his lap, and read other bits of the newspaper or a book, idly playing with his hand. I wanted this sweet scene to last forever: the two of us, in the very same country, in the very same room.

On one of these evenings towards the end of the trip, we were talking about his new apartment. "Oxford Street is such a cool location. We were really lucky to find it," Ben said. He shared the apartment with an American friend, another former member of the university fencing club.

"I'm excited for when I live here, too," I said. "It's so close to everything. I could probably walk to work if I get a job at a publishing house!"

"What do you mean?" He sounded surprised.

"Well…" I backpedaled quickly, "I mean, you know, if everything goes well, and if you get the job… I might be here by October."

"October? I was thinking more like December," Ben said.

"Oh," I was sure we'd had a version of this conversation before. "Well, if that's what you think, that's fine. I just thought you'd have time off in October after your contract ends and we could… have our honeymoon then," I said, trying to sound nonchalant.

"I'm not sure about October. I might have two weeks off in September and we could at least take a nice vacation then."

"Ben, I have a job too. If I don't marry you and move here in October, then that means I have to stay in Hong Kong and I have to *work* in September. We've talked about this." I had realized I couldn't move to London if we weren't married. Work permits for non-EU citizens were not easy to get. If we wanted to finally be together, and he had to stay in London, we would have to get married. I had thought things were going well, that it would be the right time.

"I still have no idea if I'm going to get a contract after this. I'm a little hesitant to plan our next step already." His voice softened. "Shannon, you know me. Are you really worried that I won't marry you?"

"No, it's not that at all!" I sat up to face him. "It's just I thought last year we would be together, and then it was this year, and now it looks like it's going to be next year… This isn't about a wedding or being married—believe me. It's about actually getting to be together all the time."

"I know. I want to be with you. But I need to make sure we're secure financially first."

I snorted. "I can support myself. I could even support you on my current salary." I leaned close and took his hand. "I just want to be able to do what we are doing right now every day. Once every three months isn't enough for me anymore."

I felt sick. Last year I had worked so hard to get to Hong Kong. Given up a decent job at home. Spent my last dime. Moved countries. I wanted to plan the next step. I didn't want to hang around not knowing whether or not I would be in London next year, whether or not I'd be with Ben. But he didn't have the same timing in mind. Apparently, he didn't feel the same urgency. It was time to get brutally realistic about my expectations. I wanted to plan—but Ben needed to be sure of what he wanted too.

I boarded a plane to fly away from Ben yet again. He promised to come see me during Chinese New Year. I was already counting the days. I stared at the terminal as the plane pulled away from the gate, wondering how many more airport goodbyes we'd have to endure.

When I returned to my Hong Kong apartment and looked out of the window, one of the small outbuildings in the old police complex had been demolished.

21

NEED A TAILOR, MA'AM?

Back at school the teachers were busy prepping the students for their second bout of examinations. They used my lesson times for review. I spent even more time than normal at my desk and only got to see the students at lunch recess. I missed their round faces and cheerful smiles.

In an effort to take my mind off of my inactivity and the inevitable post-Ben-visit gloom, I did some research for my sister Chelsea's wedding dress search. She was going to either purchase her gown or have it custom-made in Hong Kong. One of the perks of living in Asia was that there were tailors who would make garments from scratch at very reasonable rates. I looked for dressmakers and bridal shops online, but many Hong Kong tailors operate on referrals. The information online was often outdated or incomplete. This was a job for real life.

One afternoon I went to Tsim Sha Tsui, where my Cantonese class took place, to investigate. I exited the MTR to the tune of rushing taxis and the sparkle of the sun on steel and glass. Immediately, voices called from all sides. "Tailor? Need a tailor, ma'am? Quality suits and dresses ready for you in 24 hours!" There are hundreds of tailors in TST, mostly hawking suits and dress shirts for men and women, along with fake handbags and watches. The salesmen for these tailors accost foreigners on literally every TST street corner. Their calls are part of the rhythm of the city: "How about copy watches, ma'am? Need a handbag? Very good price! Need a tailor, ma'am?" When I was in TST I tried to walk like a local in a hurry so they would leave me alone. I had developed a curt headshake that kept the men away after their first attempt.

I went directly to one of the few shops that had been mentioned online. It was in Chungking Mansions. This was quite possibly the ugliest building in Hong Kong. Located across the street from the shiny, new iSquare shopping center in the heart of TST, it was a stone's throw from the historically posh Peninsula Hotel. Chungking Mansions was a huge building whose façade was black with filth and years of grime and further defaced by garish advertisements. It contained a plethora of tiny hotels, many of them just a few rooms each, offering extremely cheap accommodation. My dad had stayed there in the '90s for 10 USD per night—and the prices hadn't changed.

I felt nervous as I walked past the groups of men that always loitered around the entrance to the building. This was the only place in Hong Kong where I ever felt unsafe. The first floor was devoted to wholesale shops, South Asian food, foreign exchange offices and seedy-looking travel agencies. The second floor had aisles and aisles of clothing and shoe shops, nail salons, tailors and various other businesses that were somehow squeezed into 100-square-foot plots. The low-ceilinged interior was full of life and character and cheap services.

The first tailor I visited occupied the space of two of the little stalls on the second floor. I pulled open the door to find three Indian men crowded around a laptop. They sat beneath shelves stacked high with material for suits and dress shirts in every color and pattern imaginable. I cleared my throat. The fabrics filling the walls swallowed the sound.

"How can I help you?" The first man to stand up had the look of a salesman about him.

"Hi, do you make formal gowns or wedding dresses here?"

"We do, we do. How can we help you?" He went to the front desk and leaned on a glass case displaying cufflinks and silk ties.

"My sister is getting married and she'll be coming to Hong Kong to get her dress made. I was hoping you could tell me how much it might cost?"

"Let me call my salesman, he'll have that information. You know he is outside, of course?" Of course.

The first man went back to his computer, and I looked around the shop. I didn't need to move at all in order to do this because the shop was so small, but it was pristine and orderly. None of the material looked like it could be used for a wedding dress, however. I'd heard that a lot of the tailors had their work sent over to Shenzhen to keep the costs down. When the salesman arrived, he had stringy, curly hair and a navy pinstripe suit. "How can I help you today ma'am?" He gave me a toothy smile. I repeated my request for information. After hemming and hawing about how the price can vary significantly depending on the style of the dress he said, "It'll be between eight and ten thousand dollars."

That was well over 1,000 USD and it seemed like an awful lot. "And how much if I bring my own material and you only do the tailoring?"

"The actual tailoring would be more like two thousand dollars [300 USD], or maybe twelve hundred. For some we might even do it for one thousand."

"How long would it take?"

"Probably eight to ten days, with fittings to make sure it is perfect. With a dress like that it is important to be perfect. Your sister will want us to do a good job." He leered at me.

I thanked him and asked for their business card, assuring them I might be back in a few months. At least they weren't promising miracles in 24 hours. We would have to bargain them away from the 1,500 USD price-point though. I did hate bargaining.

As I stalked the aisles looking for more tailors, the salesman found me again to remind me what they could do for me. "You'll want something like that, yes?" he asked, gesturing to a shot of a wedding dress on a nearby photographer's wall. "We can do that for you, with all the beading and embroidery, anything you want." He was persistent. I nodded and ducked into another aisle to escape.

The man in the second tailor shop looked overjoyed that a young foreign woman had just walked through the doors. He stepped close, offered me a chair, leaned in. I repeated my request and he said they could do a wedding dress within 24 hours and it would cost around 800 HKD (100 bucks) including the fabric. I made a hasty exit from that shop, but not before the tailor tried to get me to have a few shirts made for myself while I was there. I did learn, however, that it was a good idea to let them know right away that I lived in Hong Kong and was not a tourist.

I felt my confidence growing as I practiced my questions and negotiations. I marched bravely into the third tiny shop, again staffed by a few South Asian men sitting around on stools. The third tailor barely looked up from his work and quoted me a price somewhere in the 800 HKD range as well. He too said it would take a mere 24 hours to finish the work.

I left Chungking Mansions and tried a few tailor shops along the road. One guy told me up front that it would be better to just buy a wedding dress off the rack. He said that of course they could do it, but he didn't seem desperate for our business.

I hadn't actually found a suitable solution to my quest, but I felt proud of myself that day. Even though I was nervous, I had spoken with half a dozen people, bargaining a bit more each time. With each passing week and new experience in Hong Kong, I was feeling more comfortable and more confident. I liked the person I was becoming in this city. Plus, I now had a fine collection of tailor's business cards.

I decided to take the Star Ferry home. It was not my first time traveling on the iconic vessel that bridges Victoria Harbour between Tsim Sha Tsui and Central, but I'd only taken it as a tourist, the first time I'd visited Ben.

The Star Ferry made the swaying journey across the Fragrant Harbour in about fifteen minutes. The MTR only took five minutes, which is why I didn't bother with the boat ordinarily, but the ferry had views. I rode in the lower deck, a mere 60 cents cheaper than the upper deck. The hard wooden seat was polished smooth by decades of passengers. I turned my face into the chilly breeze. It was a misty day, but the view of the skyline was arresting. Central stretched before me. The city climbed the backs of the verdant peaks and filled every inch of reclaimed shoreline from Kennedy Town out to Tai Koo and beyond.

I recognized many of the densely packed buildings as we rocked slowly through the spray. Iconic structures rose through the mists: the undeniably phallic IFC tower; the space station HSBC building; the white Bank of America building with red and blue trim; the twin towers of the Landmark where Ben's office used to be; the turtle-backed Exhibition Hall in Wan Chai; the golden cigarette case whose name I could never remember; the domed US Capitol-style Legislative Council building that was dwarfed by all the newer structures. In sharp relief, the piers marched along the edge of the island.

I had seen pictures of Hong Kong Island before the 1980s brought the first wave of skyscrapers to its shores. It used to look like a busy fishing village accented with white houses and a few big colonial-style structures. In those days, Victoria Peak and its cousins dwarfed the little city like rearing fire dragons. The harbor was filled with boats, large and small, that represented a healthy fishing and shipping industry. Now most of the ships made their port on the west side of Kowloon Peninsula, except for the big passenger ferries and the yachts and little junks spiriting through the water around them.

The ferry piers slid closer to me, bringing me back to the part of the city I was coming to know well. I dug my hands into my pockets and thought about the possibility of staying in Hong Kong, even alone, next year. I couldn't count on everything with Ben happening according to my timing. Maybe I *could* keep doing this on my own.

I was making progress with my co-workers. I absolutely loved the students and would feel guilty for leaving them in a year. What if they couldn't find someone else who was a good fit? I still thought wistfully of London, but I was starting to picture the barest outline of a future, at least in the medium term, in Hong Kong. I was definitely not a visitor anymore, a temporary drop in the vast sea of this city. Perhaps I was supposed to be here amidst the skyscrapers and the city lights and the flurry of languages from around the globe.

A pattern of windows filled the high-rise apartment buildings above me. It was overwhelming to think about the number of lives those squares represented, the individuals behind the glass and concrete. The different threads their lives must take all over the city filled up my mind, leaving me floating. I get the same feeling when I fly over the Phoenix metro area, where cookie-cutter suburbs stretch on and on into the desert. Phoenix looks like someone spread the buildings of Hong Kong flat across the wide open spaces.

Living in the city sometimes gave me a sinking, anonymous feeling. One person was so insignificant in the grand scheme of things. Just south of over a billion people in China, surrounded by eight million Hong Kongers, it was easy to get lost. Yet somehow I was building a life in the middle of it all—by myself.

I arrived in Central and strolled along the harbor. As I passed each pier, a list formed of all the destinations I hadn't visited yet. There were still so many things to see.

22

Lunch Adventures, Part 2

In mid-January I went down to pick up my usual tray of hot food and found the serving window in the cafeteria slammed shut. There was not a single student to be seen. It was the first day of the end-of-term exams, and I hadn't realized what that would mean for our schedule. Sometimes people didn't tell me such things, forgetting that I couldn't read any of the memos that were dropped on the teachers' desks. I wandered back to the office. Suddenly, my cheery friend Flora pounced on me from behind. "Miss Young! You go with us have the Japanese noodles! We will get the coupon again, okay! Come now, come now!"

"Okay, yes, I'll come. I'll just get my purse."

We collected Miss Lo, Jenny and the other Flora on our way out the door and headed for a taxi. It felt nice to get out of the school and be included again. There was one major difference between this and our last sojourn in a taxi: "Miss Young speaks Cantonese," announced Miss Lo from the front seat. She'd heard some of my attempts at conversation at the Christmas dinner.

"Ai-yaa?" exclaimed Flora.

I produced my latest favorite sentence in Cantonese: "*Ngoh singkei yih singkei ngh seung Guangdungwa tong!*" or "On Tuesdays and Fridays I take Cantonese lessons!"

Everyone gasped and clapped. Flora told me that I was very clever, "*hou lekh!*"

"Where do you have the Cantonese lesson?" she asked.

"Tsim Sha Tsui cheng nihn mui," I was surprised that the phrase for the Tsim Sha Tsui YMCA came so easily. She chattered to me in Cantonese. I think we talked about how long I'd been taking the class and how clever I was for trying to learn, though I can't be sure.

"Neih jung-yi mat-yeh sihk a?" she enquired.

It took me a minute. But then I got it: "What do I like to eat?"

"Yes! *Hou lekh, hou lekh!*"

"Oh, um, *ngoh jung-yi sihk* everything!" They laughed at my clumsy blending of the languages. I fumbled for more food words. "*Yum-chah!*" This is the word for going to eat dim sum, which literally means to drink tea. I also threw in the word *chasiubao* again (barbecued pork bun), amazed that I was actually having a conversation (sort of) in Cantonese in a real situation. Flora, ever the teacher, encouraged me to try out more words.

By the time we got to the restaurant I had almost run out of phrases, but Flora helped me out by asking if I wanted *chasiu mien* or *chasiu faahn* (pork noodles or pork rice). I managed to order my food in Cantonese too. Still not knowing enough of the language to make small talk, I repeated my explanation of when and where my Cantonese lessons took place for the other teachers at our table. "Miss Young *hou lekh!*" cried Miss Pong.

The first time I had lunch with this group, I'd let the words surround me throughout the meal, picking up the occasional cue from the inflections of people's voices. Mostly, I'd allowed the sounds to flow through my ears without reaching my brain. This time, I actually understood some phrases. When Flora asked the waiter for an extra bill so we could claim an extra Wellcome voucher, I knew exactly what she was saying (though that was partially through context). She insisted that *ting-yaht* (tomorrow) I should have lunch with them again.

I saw moments of triumph amongst my students sometimes too. One morning I was preparing to read a story from a big book with my weakest second grade class. I asked the class to identify the things in the cover picture of a man and his dog.

"What is this?"

"A t-shirt!"

"What color is it?"

"White!"

"What is this?"

"A hat."

"What color is it?"

"Red!"

"What is this?" I pointed to the accoutrement around the old man's neck. The boys wore clip-on ties with their uniforms in the winter, so I expected a few of them to know the word "tie".

A little boy in the front row who had not volunteered a single word in class all year suddenly took a deep breath, puffed out his chest and crowed, "Bowtie!" He collapsed back on his stool with such a look of surprise and satisfaction that I couldn't help laughing. The other students stared at him in shock, then started whispering to each other and asking what he said. He repeated the word several times for his classmates. "Bowtie!" It was the crowning achievement of his year.

An easy rhythm had developed at the school. Any time I walked through the courtyard, several young voices called out, "Good morning, Miss Young!" or "Miss Young! Good afternoon." One day I entered the elevator with Miss Wong, an English teacher, her arms full of newly graded test booklets. A group of kids shouted, "Bye-bye, Miss Young! See you later!" I waved frantically as the doors closed, hiding them from view.

Miss Wong turned to me. "They are so nice when you see them, but in the classroom sometimes they are naughty and lazy. They do not do the homework."

"I understand," I said, taken aback. "I'm sure it's frustrating when you put so much work into the classes and the kids don't always behave." I was like the fun grandparent who came in every once in a while to shower the kids with attention and presents. The regular teachers were the parents. They had to deal with the students at their worst, but I got much of their love and affection. As I got better at working with the local teachers, I came to have a greater appreciation for how busy everyone was all the time, how much pressure they were under. We didn't often vent our frustrations or get to share our funny classroom moments like teachers who shared a common language, though.

Then one day, Miss Wong took half of the students to the reading corner while I worked with the other group at the tables. Miss Wong made the students take off their shoes before sitting on the brightly colored mats. Ten minutes before the bell, the students put their shoes back on and joined my group on the little stools in front of the whiteboard to review some phonics. Before we could begin, there was a commotion in the reading corner. One of the little girls stood on the mat with a pair of white tennis shoes in her hand, looking distraught.

"Are you okay?" I asked.

She looked helplessly at me, face anxious, and then turned to Miss Wong and fired off a rapid round of Cantonese.

"These are not her shoes," Miss Wong said. I looked at the feet of the 26 other students already settling onto the stools. 26 identical pairs of white tennis shoes lined the floor.

"Uh-oh," I said, trying to keep from laughing. We spent the next ten minutes looking at the tongues of the shoes to see which ones had names written inside them by conscientious parents. Miss Wong directed the operation as most of the kids took off one of their shoes and tried to figure out if it was the same white tennis shoe they had put on that morning. The little girl with the missing shoes started to cry.

Eventually we discovered which of the students had put on the wrong shoes (there were two of them). We shuffled them around until each child wore shoes that fit. "We waste so much time," said Miss Wong ruefully as the bell rang and the students lined up to go.

Around this time, I entered the elevator with one of the young guys who worked in the office. He was new, and I assumed he was like the IT guys: reserved and inclined to use an interpreter if they had to communicate with me. I nodded awkwardly, as was my wont, and stared at the red, ascending numbers on the panel by the door.

"Where are you from?" he asked. I jumped.

"The US."

"Oh yeah? I lived in Canada for four years. You're Miss Young right? I'm Chung. I'm the new classroom assistant. How long have you been in Hong Kong?" I was shocked, and tried to recover from my earlier caginess.

"You can call me Shannon."

Chung turned out to be a gregarious communicator in English. He was around my age, and he spoke naturally, confidently. It made such a difference to be able to hold conversations at work that were not forced and formal. Soon, he was coming around to my cubicle to say hello and filling me in on all the school gossip. His aunt was a teacher at the school and had helped him get the job, so he already knew more about some of the people at the school than I did. I was thankful for his company. The other teachers had a tendency to treat me like a pet. Chung treated me like a friend.

23

A Museum, A History

At the end of January the entire school divided up into a dozen buses and spread throughout the museums and parks of Hong Kong for the annual field trip. I was assigned to the fifth grade students, who I didn't normally teach. The inevitable flurry of whispers sputtered through the aisles when I climbed onto the bus after them, followed by the whiff of exhaust from the bus. I sat across the aisle from Mr. Liu who, as usual, did not acknowledge my presence. He slept for most of the trip and not a friendly word was exchanged. Instead, I turned and stuck my head in the gap between my two seats.

"Hello! What's your name?" I said to the two shocked boys behind me.

"Uhhh, *mat-yeh-a* (what)?" They giggled and whispered to each other.

"My name is Miss Young. What is your name?"

"Oh!" one of them recognized the formula. "My name is Matthew!" he said.

"My name is Manny?" said the other.

"Manny?" I asked.

"Yes?" he said, not looking at all sure about whether that was really his name.

"Have you been to this museum before?" They exchanged glances. "The museum?"

"Oh yes. Museum," said Matthew.

"You've been to the museum before?" I pressed.

"Yes, yes, I go to the museum."

"Is it a good museum? Do you like it?"

Matthew mumbled an indistinct reply, his face turning red. He probably just didn't want to tell a teacher that he doesn't like museums. I left the poor kids alone.

Visions of the outer edges of Kowloon drifted by as we drove. I usually stayed close to the MTR when I ventured into Kowloon, so these views were new to me. Each neighborhood was different, even the ones I'd explored close to the convenient public transportation. Laundry fluttered from the sides of the buildings along the motorway. I saw the typical high-rise apartments, their bottom floors filled with shops, their upper floors decorated with advertisements. This part of the city featured older buildings whose concrete sides had been darkened by decades of heavy pollution. The clotheslines gave them life and character.

One thing that was always the same in Hong Kong was the quality of the driving. The lines that mark lanes were viewed as suggestions. From the height of our chartered bus I had an excellent view of the taxis as they squeezed in front of us with inches to spare and the minibuses as they swayed through the roads. Everyone, no matter the size of their vehicle, ignored the traffic around them. We pulled up beside a double-decker bus. I could look straight into the eyes of the people on the upper level as they passed within feet of us.

Somehow we made it to Tsim Sha Tsui without any scrapes. We pulled up to the Hong Kong Museum of History and tumbled out of the bus. I walked along the line of ten-year-olds, knowing I wouldn't be able to correct them if they stepped too far out of line. Almost immediately, a boy at the back of the line doubled over and groaned, his face turning pasty. His teacher was occupied, so I went and asked if he was okay. He didn't answer and his friends just gaped at me. I lacked the Cantonese for a crisis, so I went off to find Miss Chan. As she dealt with the stomach ache, I stood at the head of the line of kids, tapping my foot and hoping that no one else would keel over on my watch.

When we made it into the museum, Miss Chan allowed the group to disperse in each section to look at the displays. They didn't have to stand and listen to lectures or tour guides. The students ran around and touched displays all over the place and no one seemed to mind. I took this to be standard museum behavior in Hong Kong and didn't stop them.

Most of the kids flitted around like poultry, giving the displays cursory glances and quickly skipping on to each room. I, on the other hand, walked slowly, pausing to read the information and examine the bits and pieces of cultural history gathered in the museum. I knew a fair bit about Hong Kong by now, but my knowledge was fractured and concentrated on the early colonial days and the late 1950s when my grandparents lived here. The museum helped me put the pieces of the puzzle together and understand the full scope of Hong Kong's history.

Hong Kong was a fishing region that had been inhabited for centuries. The museum contained prehistoric fossils, large stuffed animals that were native to the islands, and evidence of early human activity. The earliest settlements in Hong Kong were small, but people had been present on these islands since the Stone Age. I looked at bits of pottery, tools and weapons, trying to imagine Hong Kong as a group of muggy little islands that did not matter to anyone except for the people who had carved and sculpted these items.

The region was incorporated into imperial China during the Qin Dynasty in the late 3rd century BC. It became known for fishing, salt production and pearl diving, but remained a small outpost of vast imperial China. For a brief period in the late 1200s it hosted the doomed Song Dynasty emperor as the Mongols invaded China. Even then it was a destination for refugees who came seeking work, safety and a better life.

In the early 1800s, Hong Kong was ideally situated to facilitate the burgeoning opium trade. This put it front and center when the Opium

Wars between Britain and China began. To make a long story short, Britain felt a steep trade imbalance because it imported much of its tea from China, so it began to pump opium from India into the East to make up the difference. The Chinese empire was less than thrilled to see its people becoming hooked on this dangerous, mind-clouding foreign import and demanded an end to the opium trade. Needless to say, the British did not want to lose this lucrative industry, so they went to war. The First Opium War raged between the British Empire and the Qing Dynasty from 1839-1842. Eventually, China was forced to cede strategically located Hong Kong Island to Britain after its defeat in 1842.

I felt a bit uncomfortable as I walked through the huge gallery dedicated to the Opium Wars. Weapons and even a full battleship were proudly displayed, and placards detailed the lengths to which the British Empire went to continue feeding drugs into China. It seemed a major injustice that the war happened at all. Yet the result eventually raised the profile of Hong Kong on the world stage. It was now a city that mattered. Would that still be the case if it had always belonged to China? The kids did not seem bothered by this history; Miss Chan had to stop them from climbing over a cannon in the middle of the gallery.

As the British civil servants and military officers flooded into their new colony, the city thrived. The museum depicted the old glory days of Hong Kong through a replica city street lined with teashops and dry goods stores, tailor shops and herbal medicine dispensaries. I walked through the recreated history, examining the artifacts in the shop windows as the students chased each other around the old tram car in a side gallery. Their laughter filled the artificial street. Every once in a while, one would round a display of hundred-year-old textiles and nearly bump into me. "Miss Young!" they would screech, surprised to see me wandering the museum with them.

I continued my journey through Hong Kong's history, and saw all the telltale signs of success. The British occupation brought a lot of money through the ports of Hong Kong. The more money there was, the more people thrived. British or Chinese, they pulled themselves up through their own industry in this Eastern equivalent of the Wild West.

The next great change came to Hong Kong during World War II. As the entire world was being turned around and torn apart, Japanese forces occupied British Hong Kong. The governor surrendered on Christmas Day, 1941, and the Japanese remained for three years and eight months. The museum told a story of want and imprisonment, tension and darkness that mirrored the experiences felt around the world in those days. The expats departed, hid or were shuttered in several infamous prisons, and the Chinese did what they could to appease the Japanese soldiers. When Japan's surrender ended the war in 1945, the British moved quickly to regain control before Chiang Kai-shek could snatch up Hong Kong along with the rest of China. Hong Kong had become too valuable to lose.

After the dust had settled, Hong Kong thrived again. In the post-war world, it was still poised as the gateway to the East. Victoria Harbour filled up with trade ships right away. It was during the dusty days of the 1950s that my grandparents came to Hong Kong, and most of the books I had read about Hong Kong were set in that rich and entrepreneurial age. I remembered my grandma's words: "It is a city where anything can be done, and usually is." It was a city that was ripe for business, innovation and growth.

As Hong Kong blossomed, another power was growing in the East. Red China's rise was rapid and shocking, and the bloody Cultural Revolution shifted refugees into the safe, semi-Western arms of Hong Kong. The world looked on and wondered what was going on in closed China. In America especially, there was an outcry against the Communists, but Hong Kong was more pragmatic. It felt the effects of the dramatic shifts happening within its reclusive northern neighbor, but it was firmly in the grasp of Capitalism.

In my grandmother's letters, she referenced the tenuous relationship between what was real and what was perceived about China in those days. It was all too easy for people on the other side of the world not to understand the distinction between Hong Kong and China.

It never fails to amaze me how very little the people here seem to be concerned about their proximity to the Communists. The English are, of course, in a somewhat different position, for they recognize Red China, but even the 2,000 resident Americans seldom even talk about being "worried." Every week, too, we read in the newspapers of some American concern or wealthy individuals planning to invest more and more capital into this "Pearl of the Orient." Yet, when we were home, we heard countless expressions of concern when we let it be known we were returning to Hong Kong. Many, I know, thought us foolish. (1960)

Whatever people felt about Communist China, it did not deter business from rolling into Hong Kong. Through the end of the century the city grew and grew. The first round of high-rises literally raised the profile of the city in the 1980s. Banks and businesses and high net worth individuals were attracted by the low taxes and they brought their companies and their money to Hong Kong's shores. Ever on the horizon, however, were worries that Hong Kong's eventual return to China would mean an end to this economic paradise. No one knew for certain what would happen as the 1997 Handover approached that would mark the end of the 156-year British occupation. The Hong Kong Chinese, according to the curators of the history museum at least, looked forward to their reunion with the Motherland. Preparations commenced for a new Special Administrative Region, governed under its own system but paying homage to Beijing.

The Handover took place with much fanfare, exchanges of goodwill, and assurances that Hong Kong would remain open for business. The walls of the museum were filled with portraits of the triumphant coming home of Hong Kong. Prince Charles wandered off the scene, and the propaganda filling the walls depicted a city that was happy to be rid of the British Empire.

The story in the museum ended with the Handover in 1997. This was the last plot point that registered in most people's knowledge of Hong Kong. Since then the region had been unique: one of the freest markets in the world, owned and operated by the People's Republic of China. Just like the rest of China, Hong Kong had changed in leaps and bounds in the past fifteen years. I couldn't imagine what the history books would have to say about the time of raucous economic growth I was witnessing from the inside.

I knew that for over a hundred years the influence of the West, and especially Britain, had been strong in Hong Kong. My grandma wrote that she often felt as if she was picking up more British turns of phrase than Chinese ones in her daily life. My dad claims he even had an English accent in his early years because he went to a British school.

I came to Hong Kong expecting to find a Western mark on everything. Yet a lot had changed since the Handover. I was discovering a city where the Chinese influence was pushing back the Western tide, causing the city to become more Chinese than it had been in years. The strengthening Chinese strain mixed and warred and cooperated with the long-standing Western strain, creating something unique, something modern. The disastrous condition of the US and European economies seemed to herald a shift in the order of the world. The Hong Kong of early 2011 was a vital conduit for the break-neck pace of Chinese economic growth, like a rabid, curling fire dragon, and it was fascinating to see the effects.

The final step in the museum was a video montage of great moments in Hong Kong history. When the rousing music of the Chinese national anthem played at the end, the 40 kids in the theater with me decided to sing along. I had a queer feeling of unbelonging, the same feeling I got when they sang the anthem and raised the red Chinese flag once a month at school. As much as I enjoyed getting to know the country, I was still a stranger.

24

Year of the Rabbit

I got off the MTR at Causeway Bay, one of the busiest shopping areas in Hong Kong, just before sundown. I let the crowds pull me along the street. Murmurs of excitement swarmed in the air. Huge green signs directed us toward Victoria Park. I crossed beneath a highway and entered the park. The New Year's Fair spread before me: four long aisles of stalls bursting with red and gold.

Chinese New Year is the biggest festival of the year and warrants a two-week vacation from school. Ben would be visiting me during the second week, after most of the festivities were over, so I dove into the events of the holiday by myself.

"One Way Only" signs helped control the traffic packing into the fair. Enthusiastic young people yelled through loudspeakers at the crowds, selling brightly colored plastic junk. It was the Year of the Rabbit, so rabbity things filled the stalls. There were cutesy cartoon characters and novelty toys and even an odd pair of balloons designed to look like awkwardly large breasts. The man working at that stall was wearing a pair of these anatomically incorrect creations in stony silence. The crowd bent away from this display as they flowed past.

As one of the tallest people in the crowd, I didn't have to get too close to the stalls to see their contents. People pressed around me in the throng. I was the only foreigner in sight. Teenagers selling balloons nudged each other and pointed at me when I walked by. Many expats had taken advantage of the long holiday to go to Thailand or the Philippines to sit on the beach. Some even went home to their respective countries.

The stalls of cute and kitschy things gradually gave way to the centerpiece of the New Year's Fair: the flower market. Chinese families traditionally decorate their homes with flowers during the holiday. The aroma was deeply sweet, with a tangy citrus accent. Purple blossoms are lucky, so there were countless pots of them for sale. Oranges are also lucky for the New Year, and pot after pot of orange trees trimmed in various shapes and sizes marched out of the stalls. I'd heard that at 4 a.m. on the last day of the Lunar New Year Festival, the flowers would become extremely cheap and bargain hunters would turn up in the middle of the night to buy the leftover blossoms.

At the end of the aisle, the smell of frying things mingled in the air with the potpourri aroma and festive noises. Food vendors sold fish-balls, noodles, cakes and sweets. Eating candy would guarantee a sweet year ahead. I picked out some bright, sweet morsels. As Ben's visit approached, I knew there would be more sweetness in my life soon. Objects and colors and foods dripping with symbolism filled the New Year's Fair. I wanted to take advantage of all the opportunities for luck during this holiday. I was here, in Hong Kong, and I hoped some of the luck would be transferred to me, transferred to Ben. We needed it.

The next day I thoroughly cleaned my apartment, having read that sweeping was bad luck during the New Year festival proper. I had to get it done before the festival officially began on Thursday so as not to sweep away all of my good luck for the year.

In the afternoon, Wong Tai Sin Temple tempted me with more New Year's activity. From the moment I stepped out of the MTR, I smelled incense. The heady perfume pervaded the air around the temple and seeped into my clothes and hair. I climbed a long stretch of steps past elderly women selling joss sticks and more incense. The temple was larger and more elaborate than I'd expected. Once again I was the only foreigner in the meager trickle of people. The temple's busiest time would be during the three days of the New Year Festival proper, but today was a day of preparation. Workers were setting up barriers where long lines of worshipers would gather to pay their respects and make their wishes for the year ahead. Landscapers and cleaners spread throughout the temple, polishing statues and trimming plants to prepare for the busy days ahead. There were a few other people who, like me, had decided to beat the crowds by coming the day before the festival began in earnest. I watched as they lit sticks of incense and placed them in the holders in front of the statues, bowing repeatedly as the smoke curled in front of them. In front of the largest shrine in the temple complex, people knelt, placing offerings of oranges on the ground as they paid obeisance in return for good luck in the Year of the Rabbit.

Unlike a Western church, an Eastern temple is typically open to the sky. Wong Tai Sin had a series of courtyards rimmed with colorful shrines and statues. Different sections of the temple were built on different levels. I climbed steps and wandered through the maze of the grounds, admiring the intricacies of the structure without recognizing most of the gods and goddesses represented there. There was an eerie quiet about the temple grounds despite the workers busy around me. All the worshipers were silent, and I felt like an interloper. Even the roads and apartment blocks outside the temple seemed to fade away without a sound.

Chinese New Year's Eve is the time when everyone typically eats a big meal or two with their families. The streets in Central were unnaturally quiet. In the days before the holiday, I had tried to get myself invited to someone's house for dinner. I asked Helen and June about how they would spend their holidays, asked about their families, asked about the food. I said how nice it sounded to spend the day eating and playing games at home; I mentioned my interest in experiencing Chinese New

Year for the first time—but I had no luck. Despite all of our lunchtime bonding, there was still a divide between me, the foreigner, and everyone else in my office. I thought it would be different by now. Everyone was nice and polite, but no one seemed truly comfortable with me.

During my college years in an American small town, people had routinely invited me over for dinner and offered their company in case I ever felt homesick. Even the professors occasionally had groups of students over to their homes for a meal. Although technically in the same country, my home had been 2,000 miles away—too far to travel for the shorter holidays—but there was always somewhere to go for Easter and Thanksgiving. One special couple even invited my family to stay with them during my graduation weekend. I missed that kind of warmth and hospitality here. I didn't know if this was a difference between small town and big city life, if it was a difference between American and Chinese culture, or if it was simply because I was an outsider here in a way that I couldn't be in an American town.

To avoid homesick feelings on Chinese New Year's Eve, I took myself to a movie. Truthfully, it didn't feel any different from any other evening because the holiday didn't have a lot of significance for me yet. It would just be a normal Wednesday night at home. Still, I thought about what my family would do on a normal Wednesday evening. My mom would make a dinner that people would eat in a hurry on their way to sports practices or church youth group meetings. My youngest sisters, Jamie, Olivia and Kylie, might play with the neighborhood boys in the yard or watch a movie in the living room. Later, my teenage sister Kimberly would return from fencing practice, her usual bouncy self, and tease my brother Jake while he did homework. My college-age sister Lindsay would come in with a friend or two and make a pizzookie (a big pizza cookie topped with ice cream). My brother Alex, who lived a few minutes away, might drop by if he needed to do laundry or ask for a ride to work the next day. If my dad wasn't on a business trip, he would be working on something in the garage he built himself or falling asleep while reading in the living room. I missed those typical Wednesday nights. That is what I was giving up by choosing to be here.

On the day of the New Year's Parade, I met up with Samantha in Tsim Sha Tsui. We had decided to have dinner at an Indian restaurant in Chungking Mansions before the parade. I got there first and stood on the steps looking out over the crowd that was already gathering on the street. As I rocked back and forth on my heels watching for a short blonde head, a man in dreadlocks and clothes in various combinations of yellow, green and red teetered over to me on the steps. "You are very beautiful," he leered. I whipped my phone out of my pocket, mumbled a scarlet-faced thanks and started to edge away. "What? You don't want to talk to me?" he asked trying to follow me through the crowd.

"Not really," I walked quickly down the street. I'd just relinquished the spot with the best view on the street. Fortunately, Sam pushed through the crowd at that moment. I told her about the guy as we made our way through the growing jumble of people who were jostling for the best spots by the road for the parade.

"In retrospect Chungking Mansions probably wasn't the best place to meet," she said.

"Yeah, it's just so easy to find," I said. "So, where is this restaurant?"

"I don't know. Regina told me about it. I sort of thought it would be obvious when we got here. I've never been inside Chungking Mansions."

"I guess we can just wander in and pick something. There's plenty of Indian food here."

"Sounds good! I've been dying to explore Chungking."

"It definitely isn't as much fun by yourself," I said in a low voice as we strode past the cluster of men in the entryway, one floor below the brightly lit tailor shops I had visited earlier. We passed the line to the lifts where a motley crew of backpackers was on their way to the dingy hostel rooms on the floors above.

"A girl from my town disappeared here," Sam told me.

"What do you mean disappeared?" We walked down the low-ceilinged hall, sniffing the spices from the tiny curry and samosa places tucked between signs for cheap electronics and phone cards.

"She was around our age and was backpacking around Asia," Sam began. "She was supposed to be going to Beijing with friends, and they'd even booked a trip to see the Great Wall. Then one day she decided to leave the group and bought a flight to Hong Kong. She told her family she was going to Hong Kong, and then never communicated with them again. She checked into Chungking Mansions and stayed here for one night. The hotel owner didn't see her leave. The last glimpse of her was on a security camera in Causeway Bay, where she took a couple hundred dollars out of an ATM near the train station. That was over a year ago."

"That's scary. Think she purposely disappeared? It sounds pretty intentional. How's this by the way?" We stopped at a cozy Nepalese restaurant with just six tables and checked the menu for vegetarian options for Sam.

"I can eat here," she confirmed. We entered to the warm smell of curry and spices. "I have my own theory about where she went. Let's order first." We chose our food from the extensive menu of curries and naan. A warm, yellow light filled the restaurant. There were two other groups of foreigners inside. I felt safe and cozy sitting on the wide, padded seats amidst the muted conversation and the sound of cooking drifting from the kitchens.

"So anyway," Sam continued, "this girl was really into yoga. Apparently she met some sketchy yoga people in China who told her about this yoga studio in Causeway Bay that is basically a front for a cult."

"A cult?"

"Yeah, they're really intense about having people join and they're super secretive. I went to their website and checked it out."

"Wow."

Sam leaned forward conspiratorially. "I think she's there in the studio, trying not to be seen by anyone, wrapped up in this weird community. Eddie keeps warning me not to go investigating it myself. I really want to see her and figure out why she decided to disappear without telling her family where she was going. Maybe she's been brainwashed—or drugged."

"At least she probably didn't get murdered, if that's where she is," I said. "You should solve the mystery. That would be seriously cool."

"I know. This is why I haven't been inside Chungking Mansions yet, or even gone to Causeway Bay. I've been too freaked out."

"It's so crazy that people can just go out into the world and disappear," I said. "I can't imagine breaking ties from everyone like that." I may have left my family behind—and been left behind by Ben—but so far I hadn't broken any ties. I held tightly to all of them, virtually, from far away.

When we finished our meal, we walked quickly back through the corridor and stepped out into near pandemonium on Nathan Road. The parade was starting in a few minutes and people were lined up fifteen deep along both sides of the road. We bought water from the 7-Eleven, squeezing past a group of Westerners stocking up on beer, and tried to find a place to wriggle through the crowd or stand on a fence. We had no luck on our side of the road, and crossed it using the subway tunnels to try the other side of the street. Sam was a lot shorter than me, so she had a harder time seeing over the crowd when we picked a spot. We found ourselves just opposite Chungking Mansions where we could look at the video feed of the parade on the garish screens fronting the building. We pressed against the backs of the people in front of us and tried to slide forward each time someone moved on.

As I shifted my feet between a Scandinavian family and a young Chinese couple, a very old woman suddenly appeared at my elbow. Her head was wrapped in a bright red scarf and she had an easy smile on her wrinkled face. She started pushing vigorously through the packed mass of people in front of us. Everyone gave way, even though a second ago it seemed like there was no space to breathe, much less move. We gave each other rueful smiles over her head. She disappeared beneath the crowd. A few seconds later I saw her red scarf pop out at the very front of the crowd. She had a perfect view for the parade.

As we waited for the floats, I was transported back six months to Mid-Autumn Festival. I remembered waiting for the fire dragon, alone in the crowd in the stifling heat. Now, I was waiting with my new friend to see my first lion dance, and perhaps a fire dragon thrown in. Perhaps it was going to be a lucky year.

A cheer swelled through the crowd as the music from the first float reached us. Everyone pushed in a little closer. I stood on my toes to watch the dancers cavorting through the streets. I nearly laughed out loud when the first marching band started playing a truncated version of "Bad Romance". The parade was surprisingly similar to a Western parade. The biggest difference was I didn't see any bagpipes, which are a necessary feature of parades in the Western world. The music of choice for virtually every dance group we saw was either Lady Gaga or Michael Jackson. By far the most interesting act was a Peruvian dance group that was literally dancing with scissors. I've never seen anything like it. They did all sorts of leaps and bounds and turns while waving big silver shears in the air.

Since this celebration marked the beginning of the Year of the Rabbit, almost half of the dancers, and many of the little girls in the crowd, were wearing pink bunny ears. There was something incongruously seedy about all of the bunny-eared costumes at the family-friendly parade. It looked like a Halloween party at the Playboy Mansion.

As the end of the parade neared, I worried that we had somehow missed the lion dance. This was, after all, what I was really there to see. As the Ocean Park barge passed, spraying water into the air, I looked for the Pekinese-headed lions. Finally, the official New Year float, a neon-lit, demonic-looking rabbit, rolled into view. Behind it came the lions.

A lion dance takes two people per lion. The costume heads have big fluttering ears and friendly looking eyes. Flirty fringes covering the bodies danced playfully as the lions frolicked along the street. I was surprised at how fun and life-like they were. One of the "lions" broke through the rope lining the parade route and ran up to the crowd. Everyone laughed as the security guard chased it back into line.

In the midst of the lions darted a fire dragon, dancing and twirling with a different sort of intensity. Unlike my first fire dragon, this one was sheathed in pink and purple fabric. Its Disney-esque color scheme didn't have the same menace as the Tai Hang fire dragon of Mid-Autumn. However, the frenetic energy of its movement counteracted the cuteness of the lions.

I tried to convince Sam to come to the fireworks with me the next day. She declined. I love fireworks and sometimes forget that people can be anything less than totally enthusiastic about them. I trekked down the escalator and the covered walkways to the waterfront and then meandered along the harbor with a big cup of hot chocolate. The piers were buzzing, but not completely packed. Most people watched from the Tsim Sha Tsui side. Ferry service had already ceased. I scoped out the views from the old Central Ferry Pier. Reclaimed land formed the current waterfront, so the old pier was now located about 30 feet back from the water. Piers servicing the various outlying islands spanned the space in front of the old pier like stubby toes.

In a spot that was only partially blocked by the fronds of a palm tree, I heard snippets of accents from around the world. A group of young

Germans occupied a section of the railing beside me. I tried listening to their conversation using the bits and pieces I remembered from high school Deutsch class. The cool winter night was peaceful. As the stars rose above the harbor I thought again about the possibility of spending another year in Hong Kong. I was still hoping to move to London, but this was a beautiful and unique city, with a rich culture that I'd only begun to discover. I was living a life that lots of people wish they could have. Would I end up standing in the same place to watch the same set of fireworks in one year? Was there any chance that Ben would be with me?

The first ball of fire erupted in the sky, just above one of the newer piers. The palm branches hardly obscured my view, and the balcony of the old pier in my peripheral vision made it even more magical. Because this was China, I expected some impressive pyrotechnics. I 'ooh-ed' and 'ahh-ed' at the appropriate moments and let my mind wander across the places to visit in Asia, the festivals to experience, the foods to try. Maybe it wasn't time for me to leave just yet.

25

ARRIVAL

I stood in the arrivals hall of Hong Kong International Airport, awaiting Ben's 5:20 p.m. flight. I leaned against the railing that would be the last thing that separated us—for now. Group after group of travelers walked through the opaque sliding doors and connected with their friends and relatives or pushed their baggage carts toward the Airport Express.

The clock ticked past 5:30 and I started to imagine that something had happened. What would I do if he didn't arrive?

Another five minutes passed and I tried to picture Ben retrieving his bag and hauling it toward passport control. A group of passengers that looked like they came from London strolled through the door, winter coats slung over their arms. Still, Ben did not appear on the other side of the barrier.

At 5:45 a tragic movie reel started playing in my head of waiting until the late hours of the evening and then getting a call from Ben's roommate or sister saying he had been in a terrible accident. Did either of them even have my Hong Kong number? What if he was dying of injuries after being struck by a car? What if he collapsed at work and everyone thought that someone else had told me? What if I just kept waiting by the doors and he never came through them? I pictured taking that phone call by the airport arrival gates, realizing that he wouldn't be in my life again. What would I do then? Go home?

For that matter, what would I do if Ben wasn't in my life for some other reason? Since Christmas, I'd been trying to get used to the idea that we would not necessarily be reunited at the one-year mark as we had hoped. His contract would end, but where would he end up?

As the clock struck 5:50, I tried pinching myself and saying that nothing was wrong. This was probably exactly the time it would take for him to make it out of the baggage claim anyway. There was no reason for me to think anything had gone wrong... Still I was feeling the physical effects of the worry: my skin heated up, going red. I tried to stop my hands from shaking.

It seemed that even if Ben was offered a permanent job in London, I might not be able to join him immediately. Say we waited until next Christmas. At that point I'd be just five months away from a significant two-year bonus, enough to knock out a chunk of my student loans. Could I afford to walk away from that at this point in my life?

What did I want most anyway?

Seconds past 5:55, the doors opened and Ben emerged, looking tired but completely whole. He squeezed past a small gap in the barrier and gave me a hug, just as he always does. He is a solid person. I always felt an aura of rock-solid reliability around him. "Wow, you're radiating heat. You okay?" he said, holding me at arm's length.

"Yes, just glad you're here." I pulled him close as we ambled slowly toward the Airport Express. The worry ebbed out of my body, slowly, warily. We were okay.

Early the next morning, I awoke to the sound of drums. "What's that?" I asked Ben.

"Mmmhgmrl," he muttered as he turned over in his sleep.

"Ben, wake up! What's that sound?" I shook his shoulder. The rattling, pulsing, rolling sound wasn't letting me go.

"Probably just a lion dance," he said, slipping back to sleep.

"Really?!" I hopped out of bed, my socks slipping on the marble floor as I raced to the window. People in the apartments all around me were sticking their heads out of windows, stepping out on their balconies and blinking in the morning glare.

In the courtyard beneath the building, rows of men in billowing red silk trousers beat on a row of huge golden drums. The sound echoed off the surrounding buildings and filled the dry winter sky around me. The drums beat faster. The sound tumbled around the courtyard, building, echoing and reverberating off every concrete surface. I was sure that no one behind the hundreds of windows surrounding me could possibly sleep through it.

Ben moseyed up behind me and put his arms around my waist, his voice still full of sleep. "I didn't want to miss your first lion dance."

I turned and kissed his cheek. "I saw one during the New Year's parade the other day, but this is a lot more exciting." In the courtyard beneath us I spied the lion heads on the pavement awaiting the appropriate moment. The lion dancers, two for each lion head, wore golden pants covered in a moving, shining fringe. A double row of thick, yellow poles topped with flat discs had been erected in front of the drummers, each one taller than the last. People milled about below us and found their seats in a group of chairs facing the poles, drummers and lions. A red banner rippled in the background, and beyond that the skyscrapers of Hong Kong jutted up like mismatched building blocks all the way to the harbor below.

"Who arranged all this?" I asked, watching as a group of suited dignitaries shook hands with each other and took their seats.

"Probably the building management. There are groups of these lion dancers who go all over Hong Kong through the New Year season. It's really for the kids," Ben said.

Most of the people filling the chairs were families with little children. "I still think it's cool. This is all new for me," I said happily.

Ben buried his head in my shoulder as the drummers gave one final, wild crash and silence echoed through the air. Then, the pairs of dancers raised up the lion heads, slipped underneath the tents of golden fabric and became one. The drums began once more. The lions danced and frolicked and flirted with the audience. The golden fringes glinted in the sun and gave their movements extra bits of life. One went up to a little girl in the front row and presented its head to be patted like a puppy. I watched from above as she hid her face in her mother's shirt and refused to touch the big fabric face. The lions made their way over to one of the suited men, who took a paintbrush and symbolically added the pupils to their eyes. He put a small rolled-up scroll in its wide papier-mache mouth, and the lions were off again, dancing around the courtyard to the rhythm of the drums.

As Ben and I watched, along with the little audience below, the lions climbed up onto the poles and slowly hopped from one to another. With each beat of the drums, one of the dancers hiding beneath the lion's head would jump up to the next pole, precariously maintaining his balance while still managing to look like one creature with the dancer behind him. The lions climbed higher and higher. Somehow, even though they were balancing atop narrow poles, they had enough poise to make the movements of the lions seem real. The head of one of the lions finally reached the highest pillar. With a final drum roll, the lion dropped one end of the scroll. It was nearly the length of the pillar and unfurled all the way to the ground. The crowd applauded wildly.

"What does the scroll say?" I asked

"Messages of good luck for the New Year," Ben answered. "Are you happy?" he asked.

I kissed his cheek as we turned back towards the apartment. "Definitely."

26

MACANESE TREASURES

"Want to see the Fishbowl?" Ben asked. We were winding our way between the casinos of Macau, a neighboring peninsula and islands tacked onto the edge of China. The sun was shining, reflecting off steely, garish casinos and the white concrete around us. Women wearing sun visors like giant duckbills shouted in Mandarin. Men laughed and smoked, sending gray tendrils above the crowds. Taxis zoomed past the casinos, jockeying for position.

"What's the fishbowl?" I asked.

"You'll just have to see." He guided me toward the Lisboa, an old hotel and casino that sat in the shadow of its newer incarnation, The Grand Lisboa. The old Lisboa looked like an elongated cake, its rusty orange structure all trimmed in white. The Grand Lisboa, on the other hand, was shaped like a giant pineapple. The yellow and blue panes of glass covering the surface made it look like a giant disco ball that had gone to seed and started sprouting.

Macau, a Special Administrative Region returned to China from its Portuguese colonial overlords, is the Las Vegas of the East, the prime gambling location in Asia. It is a short hydrofoil ride from Hong Kong, and the ample shopping and eating options make it a popular destination for Hong Kong tourists. And Chinese people love to gamble. The casinos attract very high rollers and supposedly bring in five or ten times the revenue of the Las Vegas strip. But, like Vegas, Macau has a sinister side.

Ben guided me to the older Lisboa, which was still bustling despite the grandeur of its fruit-shaped cousin. Priceless jade and ivory sculptures and Ming dynasty vases decorated the lobby. I stopped—in awe—to look at the intricate carvings and paper-thin vases. Every single one would have been at home in a museum. "These are all owned by the Chinese gambling tycoon who built the Lisboas," Ben told me.

"Is this fishbowl another priceless treasure?"

"Not exactly. It's this way." We descended into the depths of the building on a long escalator and found ourselves in a corridor crossing between the old and new Lisboas and then made a circle in the depths of the pineapple building. Pulsing cafés, club-like restaurants and little shops lined the corridor, inside and out. They were mostly filled with men. Circling slowly around the corridor were scores of girls. I would have liked to call them women—all of them may have been over eighteen—but they all looked like tiny teenagers. As if they were playing at a roller rink, they went around and around, wearing tall heels and short, tight dresses. Scooping necklines glittered with rhinestone jewelry beneath powdered faces. They circled the corridor in packs. Men watched from seats in the cafés.

"Do you see why it's called the Fishbowl?" Ben asked. His thick eyebrows were drawn low over his eyes.

"Are they prostitutes?" I asked, my voice rising.

"Yes."

"Where do they all come from?" I asked, looking back at the parade of women, thinking about my six sisters.

"They're mostly Mainland girls who need a way to make money. Sometimes they come here with recruiters, thinking they'll be doing something else. For some, it's a more glamorous way to make a living than working in a factory."

"They look so young!" I watched a group teeter by me on their heels. The smallest girl wore a draped royal blue dress that was cinched at the waist with a wide black belt that ended just a few inches above her short hem. Her round face would not have been out of place in the 9th grade, except for the sparkling fake eyelashes. I tried not to watch as two girls started talking to a paunchy man sitting at the edge of the ring of human traffic. They giggled at his comments. One put a small, pale hand on his arm.

"Is prostitution legal in Hong Kong?" I asked.

"Prostitution is but brothels and public solicitation are not," Ben answered. He gestured to the corridor. "In Macau things are a little more open. My mum was the one to show me this, actually, thought it was important for me to understand. Personally, I think the men are disgusting, but I thought you might be interested. All this wealth in China right now has a dark side."

"Thanks for showing me," I said. "Can we go now?"

As we rode the escalator out of the pit of the Fishbowl, I thought about the ease with which I made a living—thanks to where I was born. Sure, I was in debt, but that was because I had decided to purchase an expensive education. And I was able to make my payments every month. Most of the women strutting through that circular gauntlet probably sent money home to their families, just as the girls who worked in China's massive factory towns did. I'd never needed to send money to my family. Would I don short skirts and parade around for men sitting at the windows of basement restaurants if I too were providing for my parents back home? For my grandparents? For my brothers and sisters? Was this a better life than that of a migrant worker in a Chinese factory town?

We returned from the bowels of the pineapple and went into different casinos at random. Gold dripped from the walls, the chandeliers, the mirrors. The entire place was newer and more opulent than Las Vegas. Everything from the carpets to the ornately carved reception desks in the casinos looked costly. One lobby boasted a wall-to-wall aquarium filled with the flashing colors of koi and clown fish. The entire place felt grotesque after what we'd just seen.

Ben tried his hand at blackjack. "I usually come out ahead in Macau," he muttered as he surrendered the last of his chips to the house. I poked at the slot machines and played an automated roulette game, but mostly I watched the people who filled the tables and milled about in the smoky rooms. The majority of the gamblers were Chinese, but a few Europeans and other nondescript Westerners wandered through the crowds. The people looked nothing like the Americans who populate Vegas casinos wearing casual jeans and Disney t-shirts and feeding slot machines from plastic Gatorade cups. These gamblers dressed in smart, somber colors with shiny, polished shoes. They didn't smile when they played, crowding intently around the tables and staring down at their cards and chips. They made diligent notes on bits of paper as they analyzed the game. They did not make it look fun. Gambling was serious business in Macau.

Ben told stories about coming here as a child. He pointed out the most famous hotels and told me about the extravagant casino tycoons who'd built them. I felt very small as we wandered between the huge lobbies and gambling rooms. The atmosphere was oppressive in a desperate sort of way—but also fascinating. When the heady, smoky opulence became too much we stumbled out into the sunshine. "Can we go see some Portuguese stuff now?" I asked.

Ben laughed. "Sure. You didn't like it?"

"I don't understand how people can dump their money like that."

"It's all about luck and superstition. Chinese people love gambling. Plus," he added offhandedly, "it's a convenient way to launder money. That's the real reason so much cash goes through here."

Outside, we disappeared into the narrow, European-style streets. Whereas Hong Kong still bore signs of British rule, Macau tasted of Portugal. We dodged vespas and tramped up cobblestones. We visited mission churches and tried the famous Macau egg tarts: warm, creamy custard encased in crumbling pastry crusts. The Portuguese influence bloomed in every street. The houses were painted in blues and yellows and soft, faded reds. Verandas sloped from the upstairs floors of the houses and laundry fluttered from the railings like broken lace fans.

We found our way to the top of an old fortress, now a museum, where we had a view of the sprawling, run-down city. Casinos rose luridly above slums. Grimy lean-tos and rickety apartments, more derelict than you would see in Hong Kong, stumbled across the peninsula. Macau was a city of contrasts. But there were breathtaking moments of beauty as the sun flashed off the shiny casinos and the light played between the narrow streets. After the confusing, burdened stimulation of the casinos, I felt renewed by the fresh breeze and the soft colors. Ben took my hand. We climbed back down the fortress and continued to wander together through this new part of the world.

My grandparents visited Macau with their children long ago. In those days Macau was still part of Portugal, just as Hong Kong was still part of Britain. Their letter home made me realize how much this part of the world had changed in the last 50 years.

Early this year, our family enjoyed a 3-day vacation in Macau, the interesting little Portuguese province just three hours from Hong Kong by ferry [it only takes an hour these days]. Even Craig, who was just six months old at the time, seemed to thoroughly enjoy himself. We stayed at a charming little Portuguese-styled inn, where we especially enjoyed the fine meals. We learned, contrary to our expectations, that Macau is not a bustling city of gambling and intrigue as it is so often painted. True, there is a good bit of both connected with this place, but it is not evident to the casual visitor. Instead, it is really a quiet, almost lazy, town with few cars, many pedicabs and easy-going, somewhat lackadaisical but polite public servants. Much of the architecture to be seen is Portuguese, making this sleepy little place a bit of old Europe in the middle of the Orient.

On this tour we were taken, a little too close for comfort, I will readily admit, to the very edge of No Man's Land, the swampy area separating Macau from Communist China. We were no more than 500 yards away from a Red pillbox with a sentry patrolling about. There were other sightseers there at the same time who were anxious to take pictures—something we had been told was frowned upon. A "border incident" was all my sometimes dramatic imagination could picture! At any rate, I was happy to leave that spot. Actually, though, it is across this swamp where, monthly, hundreds of Chinese, under cover of darkness, escape from their homeland. An astonishing percentage of Macau's population is made up of refugees who have fled from China. Former rich and poor alike live in an area of simple dwellings provided by the Macau government. We were also taken to the official gateway to China, marked by an impressive archway patrolled by Portuguese and Communist soldiers on either side. Despite these few moments which reminded us just how far away from home we actually are, we very much enjoyed our stay in Macau and returned to busy, overpopulated Hong Kong quite rested and refreshed. (1961)

Ben told me it was still true that Macau was a haven for refugees. They have been less strictly regulated than those coming into Hong Kong, making it a place for the desperate. When Macau was ready to be handed back over, rumor had it that China did not want it back. Famous for hosting poverty and corruption, all the money flowing through the casinos was not enough to help the region recover fully.

Like my grandparents, we were happy to return to our busy, overpopulated Hong Kong. We spent most of the week sleeping in, eating, wandering around the city—simply being together. He told me stories of his childhood in Hong Kong, how his hours had been allocated to piano lessons, homework and Latin tutoring. He pointed out the apartment buildings his family had lived in over the years, brought me to the rundown mall in Wan Chai where he used to buy comics, lamented the disappearance of the food court from Pacific Place. For a few days, I had a glimpse of what this year could have been like, the kind of explorations we could have enjoyed together.

When we said goodbye beneath the fluorescent lights of the airport, we didn't realize how long it would be until we saw each other again. Our longest separation ever had begun.

27

TOWN AND GOWN

Barely a week after Ben went back to London, Chelsea and Francois flew in from Korea. They had just finished their teaching contracts and were beginning their worldwide wedding tour. They would be married first in South Africa with Francois's family and again in America with ours. They still had not met most members of each other's families... or any of their old friends. I was one of the few who got to bridge the gap.

Chelsea and Francois marveled at how international Hong Kong was. "You have H&M here? I love H&M!" Chelsea would squeal as we walked down Queen's Road. Right away, they loved the melting pot of the streets and the mixture of old and modern. At nearly every street corner, they would exclaim over a familiar chain restaurant or shop.

"Look, there's a Pizza Express. I remember those from when I lived in England," Francois said as we climbed the cobbled streets of NoHo.

"One of the reasons we got so tired of Korea was it was hard to find anything familiar," Chelsea told me. "But it's all here."

"It's almost cheating," I said. "Sometimes I feel guilty for going to Western-style businesses instead of local places, but the locals go to them too." I felt proud of my world city as we visited my favorite spots: Holly Brown, Nha Trang, Bacar.

Our number one priority, though, was to find Chelsea a wedding dress. Just nineteen days remained until their small wedding ceremony in South Africa. We had finally given up on the tailor idea because designing a wedding gown intimidated us both. We decided to see what we could find on the racks.

We spent the first evening going into bridal shop after bridal shop along Kimberley Road in Tsim Sha Tsui. Although Hong Kong girls had adopted Western dress styles for their weddings, they did not share our preference for white dresses. Half of the dresses were white or ivory and the rest were every color from bright red to pale yellow to deep purple to iridescent green to turquoise with sparkles. Hong Kong brides also didn't seem to be charmed by anything 'simple' or 'elegant'. The dresses were princess ball gowns covered in bows, frills, rhinestones and frothy details. Where an American girl might choose a Cinderella dress with a simple sash or an elaborate skirt detail paired with a simple bodice, the Chinese girls seemed to want dresses with as many embellishments as possible. This is jarring enough in white: in fuchsia it was shocking. The sales people were used to Westerners and their tastes. As soon as we walked in they would say, "You are looking for something simple, right?"

Chelsea wanted a strapless dress with a gathered detail at the front and a simple train. As we looked at racks full of frothy creations, she became less sure of what she wanted. She tried on all sorts of dresses, trying to figure out which styles looked best on her. I tried some on too. We cajoled each other to put on some of the "Hong Kong styles." We paraded in front of tri-paneled mirrors and offered each other sisterly opinions. I loved the silk dresses overlaid with lace, ran my fingers over satin sashes and belts.

Chelsea's a thin woman, but she is 5'9". And I mean thin by American standards, not Chinese. We had difficulty finding dresses that fit. The sales girls had to pin extra pieces of fabric in the back of some dresses so we could see what they would look like after being let out. We told the salesgirls that Chelsea's wedding date was two weeks away. Universally, their eyes would go wide.

"Aiy-aah! So soon!"

"Many girls come in one year before!"

"You need it very fast, la. You buy today."

In Hong Kong, brides don't usually buy their wedding dresses. They wear several gowns throughout the course of the wedding, including a traditional cheongsam and an evening gown for the reception. They rent dresses for their pictures, which are not usually taken on the day of the wedding. Couples in prom-worthy attire being followed about by sweaty-faced photographers are a common sight at scenic locations like the Pottinger Street steps and 1881 Heritage Square in Tsim Sha Tsui, even on weekdays. Brides often book their wedding gowns in a package with hair, make-up and photography services included, and then leave the dress behind when the pictures are done. But we were there to buy, and it was harder than we expected.

The shops stayed open late, but as 10:00 p.m. came and went we became frustrated. In one shop that still had lights on, we were surprised to find three brides still trying on dresses. They discussed the gowns with their mothers and looked at pictures of hair and make-up designs. We squeezed over to some chairs and looked through the book of pictures to see if there was anything that appealed to us, then waited our turns for the dressing room. The girl next to us was showing her mother a bright red ball gown worthy of a Disney princess in the final act.

Chelsea and I felt lucky to get to shop for wedding dresses together, even though our mom couldn't be there with us. Going abroad often means that you relinquish your rights to family time. I had to miss birthdays and anniversaries and even weddings. Hopefully the other people in my life understood why I was not there. In 1955, our grandmother got married in Japan in a white dress that she had brought with her for parties. She had a few kids by the time she made it home to introduce her new husband to her parents. At least Ben and Francois had been able to meet our parents by now.

When a dressing room became available, I went first. I had been trying on dresses for fun and figured it wouldn't hurt if I bought one. When else would I be able to go wedding dress shopping with family? My mom was 3,000 miles away, and I had my globetrotting big sister with me. For once, I didn't need to be pinned into the dress. It was a bit too tight, but the zipper closed all the way. I walked to the mirror. The dress was a beautiful ivory silk, overlaid with a subtle lace pattern. It was strapless and tight to the hips, where it flared in a shower of embroidery and tiny pearls. There was a pale pink bow around the middle and it had a train crusted with lace and little pearls like a crisp edge of frost. Everyone in the shop turned to admire it, or so I imagined. I looked great.

I twisted and turned and looked at the dress from all angles, turned red, giggled. Then I dug my toes in and argued the price down from 8,000 HKD (over 1,000 USD). It wasn't until the price went below 6,000 HKD that I realized what a good bargainer I had become. We asked the shop to hold the dress until the next day so I could think about whether I was really going to buy a wedding dress before getting engaged.

Of course, we were there for Chelsea. She found a gown that she liked, but it was about 1,000 HKD more than mine. The salesgirl didn't seem to like it anyway, and kept trying to talk Chelsea into considering different styles. She pulled out a dress with a big princess skirt, fluffed up with tulle and crusted with rhinestones on the bodice. The mid-section was made from transparent netting. I insisted that Chelsea try it on. It looked really good on her, and she twirled in front of the mirror. "It's so see-through!" she said.

"You can put a piece of fabric there to cover your stomach. It is very beautiful," the salesgirl told her.

"That would defeat the purpose of the dress," I said.

Chelsea laughed. "I don't think this is quite what I'm looking for."

As she spun once more in front of the mirror, I glanced at the big picture windows that opened onto the street. A middle-aged European couple was standing on the other side of the glass, watching the fun. They put on huge smiles and gave her the thumbs up as if to say, "Yes! That one's perfect! Choose that dress." Chelsea declined.

By the time we finished giving our names and collecting business cards from the shop, we were tired. The rest of the shops on the wedding dress street looked closed. Empty-handed, we headed in the direction of the MTR. We passed one more shop window that still had its lights on. Chelsea glanced inside and stopped dead. "It has a gathered waist!" There was a dress in the window in the style she wanted, along with a pretty sprinkling of embroidery. It had a long train and it was the bright white color Chelsea had been looking for all evening. The woman in the shop told us that it was too late to go over to the showroom and try on the dress. We promised to come back.

While we had been shopping, Francois met a tailor on the sidewalk and had a dashing new suit made. He said the tout had been shocked when he called out, "Need a tailor, sir?" and Francois agreed to go along with him to the shop without hesitation.

Chelsea and I were feeling the pressure: she had to leave to get married in just a few days, and we still didn't have a dress for her. The next day, I got home from work late and we didn't have time to go back and try on the dress Chelsea had seen. We went to a big, cramped wedding mall in Prince Edward where we hoped the gowns would be within our price range. We did find cheap dresses, but there were even fewer options in our size and style ranges. We didn't find anything that was quite right. Then in the last shop, amidst bright purple and turquoise fluff, we found one workable dress. It was nice. It had a long train and pretty embroidery, but something wasn't quite right. It looked good on Chelsea, but she wasn't excited about it. "I feel like this is just *a* dress but not my dress, not *the* dress I want to walk down the aisle in."

The woman who worked in the shop was anxious to make the sale. "I take the measurements." She shouldered past me.

"I'm not sure it's the one I—," Chelsea started to say.

"You have only five days. I take the measurements now."

"Maybe we can come back later," I said.

"No time. Put arm up."

I could see Chelsea was starting to feel flustered. The woman kept talking about all the time it would take to do the alterations and how we had to make the purchase tonight. "Next time you come one year in advance. No time. No time." She wrapped a faded tape measure around Chelsea's waist.

"We don't want this one," I said finally. "We will come back if we change our minds." The woman gave me a disgusted look and turned away. Chelsea struggled out of the dress and we left the shop. The gates to the wedding mall had already been closed and we had to slip through a side door to escape.

By the third day, we were trying to avoid panic. The twittering warnings of the salesgirls who thought we had waited far too long to start shopping were playing on repeat. We rushed back to Kimberley Road to try on the dress from the window. The size was right, the price was close enough to right, and even the lady in the shop was nicer than the one from the night before. The gathered waist flattered Chelsea's tall, thin frame. The bright white silk train filled the little carpeted dressing room. We threw in a silver-edged veil, paid the bill and breathed a huge sigh of relief.

Then, we returned to the other shop and purchased my dress too. I lived on the other side of the world from my mom; this was a chance to buy a wedding dress with my sister. With no idea when or if I'd be getting married, I figured I might as well get it over with! I'd taken enough risks for Ben already. What was one more gamble that everything would work out?

Saturday morning dawned triumphant. We had just purchased wedding dresses, after all. Chelsea, Francois and I caught the ferry to Lamma, an outlying island I hadn't visited yet. The hydrofoil ferry was full when we got to the pier, so they brought in a backup "slow ferry" that had probably been in commission for at least 50 years. I wondered if my grandparents ever rode on the same ferry. It meandered out of Victoria Harbour and around the western edge of Hong Kong Island. The cityscape gave way to thick green vegetation growing all the way down to the waterline. We arrived on Lamma about 45 minutes later. The ride takes less than half an hour on the regular fast ferry, making it possible for people to indulge in the conveniences of the city and commute to Central every day while still enjoying an idyllic island lifestyle.

We disembarked and immediately took in deep breaths of sea air. We smelled salt and mud, fish and smoke on the breeze as we walked down the long concrete pier toward Yung Shue Wan village. Gulls rode the wind above us. Hundreds of bicycles lined the pier, perhaps left behind by people who had taken the ferry into Central that day.

There are two main villages on Lamma, with a paved path running between them. Visitors could take the ferry from either end. One village was famous for its seafood restaurants, and the other for its quirky shops. We were visiting the latter.

Children ran through the street. We took pictures of boats and bicycles and wandered the streets, popping into little tourist shops every hundred yards or so. We had to turn aside for friendly packs of dogs and old men pushing carts piled high with vegetables. Lamma is downmarket from the residences on Lantau Island—which includes the San Diego-like Discovery Bay—making it a refuge of hippies and free-spirited expats. It was amazing that such a sweet little island village could exist so close to the madness of central Hong Kong.

It turned out that Francois liked to shop, too. We took our time choosing handmade earrings (two pairs for 2 USD) and gifts for our family. Incense, colorful woven fabrics and miscellaneous handicrafts surrounded us. The colors filled our eyes as purchases filled our hands.

Eventually, we wandered away from the shops and climbed the main path leading out of the village. Big, twisted banyan trees shaded the walkways and locals, tourists and expats mingled in the open-air restaurants and in the streets. "You guys should move to Hong Kong and live here," I said. "I could totally picture you doing the laid-back island lifestyle."

"I could be happy living here," Francois said. Their current plan was to spend the summer in the US and then look for teaching jobs in an exciting new country, hopefully in the Middle East.

A Chinese man called out from his balcony to an Englishman in the street below who was dragging a carry-on sized suitcase. "Hello Harry! Where are you going?"

The man in the street replied, "Off for a spot of shopping. We'll be back this evening."

"Very good. Very efficient!" said the man above as he went back to his newspaper and cup of tea.

"It's so friendly here," I continued. It would be so much fun to have my sister and soon-to-be brother-in-law so close by. I imagined all the beachside barbecues we could have beneath the sub-tropical sun.

We followed the path past village houses and makeshift shops. Eventually the road climbed and dipped into a thick grove of trees and typhoon-twisted undergrowth. We saw terraced houses surrounded by banana trees and satellite antennas. There was a steady stream of amblers on the path. Chelsea and Francois were thoroughly charmed by the island. I continued trying to talk them into taking teaching jobs in Hong Kong. I pictured spending long weekends on the porch of their village house, sipping Tsingtao beer and watching for snakes.

The path gave way to a Chinese restaurant advertising famous pigeon dishes closely followed by a beautiful beach. The foliage opened up just enough to make way for the sand and the rocks and the sun. A sign that read "Welcome to This Beach" immediately confronted us.

"This beach, eh?" Francois asked.

I laughed. "Not just any beach, welcome to *this* beach." We took pictures with the sign and scrunched over the sand. We found a spot near the rocks at the edge of the beach and sat down on the sand. It was just warm enough. The beach must become crowded in the summertime, but we shared it only with an elderly Chinese couple and a few quiet families. I visualized Chelsea and Francois's newlywed life on Lamma Island. Ben was with me in my imagined casual beach weekends.

"Are you guys nervous about getting married?" I asked. "It seems so soon to me."

"Not really," Chelsea replied, screwing up her face against the sun. "We've spent practically every minute together for the last two years. I don't think it will make that much of a difference."

"Are you nervous, Francois?"

"No, I guess I'm not." He reclined in the sand, at ease with the changes on their horizon. I wondered if the life I'd eventually lead with Ben would have the same easiness as theirs. Did it have the same inevitability?

After we had soaked up as much sun as Lamma had to offer on a fine March day, we returned to the village for seafood and fresh island vegetables. At a table right by the water, we listened to the easy rush and flow of the tide. Around us, locals and travelers cracked open shrimp and passed around pots of tea and tall bottles of beer. As I ate fresh vegetables and garlic-encrusted shrimp, I couldn't imagine being anywhere else in the world.

28

LITERARY FESTIVITIES

As my life in Hong Kong filled up, I held on to my earlier dreams of working in the book industry one day. As much as I enjoyed chatting with my students, I was desperate to talk about books with anybody who read something besides *Good Choices for Cat and Dog* and *Five Green Monsters*. Then, I discovered the Hong Kong International Literary Festival, a ten-day series of lectures, seminars and social events with dozens of notable authors. The literary world in Hong Kong was still a mystery to me, so I offered my services as a volunteer at every event that was not happening during school hours. For a few events, I was assigned the enviable duty of "author escort".

My first job was Peter Hessler.

I left Chelsea and Francois packing up the last of their stuff in my apartment and hiked up the Escalator into Mid-levels, to the apartment building where Peter Hessler was staying with his family. An American journalist known for his coverage of China as the Beijing correspondent for *The New Yorker*, he had written three books on China, including *River Town*, a terrific travel memoir about his two years teaching in a local college.

I arrived in the lobby early, my palms sweating from more than just exertion. In addition to being star-struck by authors in general, I had just finished reading Peter Hessler's book the day before. In *River Town*, he comes off as a really nice, personable guy. Still, I was nervous. Using the number given to me by the event organizer, I called to let him know I was in the lobby. *The* Peter Hessler was listed as one of the contacts in my cell phone! True, it was probably just the number of the apartment where he was staying, but I felt proud nonetheless.

When he walked into the lobby, he was shorter and slighter than I expected. His dark brown hair had a hint of gray. He was tired, having arrived from the US the night before with his wife, author Leslie T. Chang, and their nine-month-old twins. We hailed a cab in Mid-levels and talked about Hong Kong, about Beijing, about where we were from in the States. He seemed genuinely interested in asking about me and my life. How did I end up in Hong Kong? What were my opinions of the education system? He was intrigued that I was teaching in a local school. He wanted to know more about how much the kids studied and how much they were allowed to be creative in their schoolwork. I could see why his subjects felt comfortable telling him about their lives.

We arrived at the speaking venue: the Royal Geographic Society. I went off to take tickets and the elderly expatriate crowd surrounded Peter Hessler. They waved champagne glasses in bejeweled hands and asked questions in loud voices. As the audience began to take their seats, he came over to chat with me again, as if he felt just as out of place among the old boys and expat wives as I did. Were Peter Hessler and I friends now?!

When the event began, I stood in the back and listened. Hessler was at ease in front of the audience, cracking jokes and showing jaw-dropping pictures of the northern Chinese landscape. His latest book, *Country Driving,* included stories about a road trip along the remote stretches of the Great Wall during which he stopped to pick up rural hitchhikers and talk to people in the villages. China was in a state of constant change, and Hessler witnessed firsthand the rapid migration of people from the villages to the cities. The majority of the workers on the move were women, all searching for a better life in the big factory towns. People with very little exposure to the outside world were about to jump headlong into the progress machine of modern China, and he was there to talk to them. Hessler saw the evidence of a breakneck rate of change everywhere, from the modern roads to the cell phone carrying villagers to the brand-new factory towns standing empty as they waited for occupants. I was witnessing the effects of this upheaval too.

I thought about the parents of the students at my school. So many of them were recent immigrants from Mainland China, members of this massive migration. They wanted a better life for their kids, and I hoped that in Hong Kong they had found it. It was exhilarating to be a witness to this major shift in the biggest country in the world. In my own way, I was seeing the effects of change firsthand through the families themselves.

Hessler said that he learned the most about being a writer from his time teaching in China. Studying literature at Princeton and Oxford paled in comparison to studying people in a remote river town. I could relate to this sentiment, although Hong Kong was hardly remote. Nothing had taught me to keep my eyes and ears open for the people around me like living in a brand-new city on the other side of the world. I felt inspired as my new friend spoke. It made me want to share my small side of this story too.

The literary festival spanned a weekend, and Saturday was jam-packed with events. I was determined to be the best volunteer ever, wondering if it could help me gain entry to the world of editors, authors and publishers in Hong Kong. I'd thought that dream was only possible in London or New York. Could it happen in Hong Kong instead?

I made my way to the Hong Kong Racing Museum for a bevy of events. The setting proved to be perfect as the authors arrived and shared their experiences, advice for aspiring writers, musings on their work. In between collecting tickets and informing spectators when the events were due to begin, I snuck away for a quick bite to eat. I walked over to the famous dim sum restaurant adjacent to the Racing Museum with one of the head volunteers, a red-haired Frenchman who sported a black turtleneck and a sexy accent. Philippe had followed his girlfriend, a teacher, to Hong Kong, where he had become a professional volunteer. When I told him of my own efforts to follow a lover to Hong Kong, he surmised: "Such is modern love."

The big picture windows looked out on the Happy Valley Racecourse, a Hong Kong institution. The festival organizers had booked a table for the day to make sure the authors and volunteers could eat. At the table, we found Rajeev Balasumbramanyam, the author who had just finished speaking, along with his partner Divya and fellow Hong Kong-based author Manreet Sodhi Someshwar. Rajeev was an Indian author who looked a little like Jesus and grew up in the UK. He had made a name for himself by writing a poetic literary novel called *The Dreamer* at age nineteen. The three of them were just tucking into the plates of spring rolls and bamboo steamers filled with dumplings and were happy to have us join them. I couldn't believe my luck. They told stories about their first few years as writers in Hong Kong. I had to remind myself to eat between moments spent gaping at them. They were just so cool.

"So where are you from, Shannon?" Manreet asked, her warm smile reassuring me.

"The US. Arizona."

"Really?" Rajeev leaned forward in his seat. "I've always been fascinated by that part of the States. The desert and the wide open spaces. There's an interesting mystique that surrounds that whole area."

"I guess there is," I said. "You appreciate it more after you leave, I think." It is true that the sky is bigger out West. The blue expanse fills more than its share of space, interrupted only by jagged mountains at the edge of the desert. Rajeev fired off a round of questions about the world where I grew up. I knew that Arizona was mildly interesting, but not to a group of internationally recognized authors. They had been to exotic places, fascinating places, yet they were asking for my stories.

I told them about the road trip Ben and I had taken the summer after my university graduation. We drove from Phoenix to San Diego, stopping in Laguna Beach to dabble our feet in the ocean. We went to Los Angeles, where we stood still in traffic in my sister's beat-up little car, walked the Avenue of Stars, and drove as close to the Hollywood sign as we could get. We sped across the desert to Las Vegas, which was exciting and colorful and unreal. We even watched a topless cabaret show where the girls wore huge feathered headdresses.

As Manreet, Rajeev, Divya and Philippe listened, I spoke of our trip north through the empty center of Nevada, where our tire blew out 50 miles from the nearest outpost of civilization and Ben had to change it beneath the dramatic, blue mountains. Ten miles later the spare blew out too, and we rode the rims until darkness and a burning smell convinced us to use the last drop of power in my cell phone to call a tow truck. I told my new friends how we spent two days in Battle Mountain, Nevada while a shady mechanic replaced our wheel and ordered parts to fix our twisted rims and repair our stripped brakes. We wandered the desolate town and spent long hours in the diner and the lonely milkshake shop.

"Did any of the locals invite you to their homes for dinner?" Rajeev asked as he leaned forward over his bowl of fried rice. Alas, they did not.

"I sort of hoped something like that would happen. It would be a cool story," I said.

Rajeev looked disappointed. "I picture people in small towns being a lot friendlier." He glanced out the window at the skyscrapers rising above the racetrack.

"Yes, but we were still outsiders. I can understand why they weren't that welcoming."

"Sometimes Hong Kong is like that too," he said. "It's a strange city."

"How did you get home?" Divya asked.

After we finally escaped Battle Mountain, we drove through the impossibly green southern section of Idaho and visited the Idaho Potato Museum. Finally, we made our way to Salt Lake City where we fenced in a tournament together. We toured the Mormon Temple and then drove south through the red rocks of Utah and the dry, green desolation of northern Arizona before finally arriving at home.

"That sounds like a life-changing trip," Manreet said.

"Would you consider writing about it?" Rajeev asked.

Could I?

They were also interested in my work at the school. Divya said she knew teachers at international schools, but in a year in Hong Kong she hadn't met anyone who worked in a local school. "What is it like? Do you get along with your co-workers?" she fixed her piercing brown eyes on mine.

"To be honest, it can be a little bit isolating," I said. "Most of them can speak English, but it takes a lot of effort and they're really busy so they don't talk to me that often."

"Have you been able to connect with other expats?" Manreet asked. She had been in Hong Kong a lot longer than the other two.

"Yes, I've made friends with some other NET teachers and that's helped a lot."

"That's good. When we first arrived it took us a while to meet people too. I'm glad you found a support group." I envied Manreet's worldly demeanor. Would I be like her after another few years in Hong Kong? *Would I be in Hong Kong another few years?*

I was inspired by the way these writers and Peter Hessler saw a story in everything and drew on the experiences of everyone around them. I wanted to be around more people like that, to follow their example. I left with the seed of an idea for a story about Hong Kong.

When the literary festival drew to a close I was filled with a new energy. I was starting to see Hong Kong as a city where I might find fulfillment, not only by satisfying my sense of adventure and desire to try new things, but by providing the opportunities that could sustain and challenge me in other ways too. I didn't want to be a teacher forever, but as the festival ended, my mind filled with ideas. I could get to know the literary people in Hong Kong, find out where they were hiding amongst the dim sum restaurants and skyscrapers, maybe even work in publishing after all. The English-speaking market might be smaller here, but the people seemed fresher and more entrepreneurial than in London and New York, where austerity measures were choking the business. If all else failed, I could take over the literary festival.

At the closing party of the literary festival, held amongst the dark wood tables and ornately latticed windows of The Pawn restaurant in Wan Chai, I met expats who had been in Hong Kong since 1991, '92, '93. Most of them said they intended to stay for a few years. They came with husbands or signed two-year contracts. They saw it as a place to live for a few years, a place to have adventures, not a place to live forever. But they had never left.

29

TEA AND TWENTY-SOMETHINGS

Workers had been drilling holes in the concrete courtyard of the old police complex. There were new square depressions every time I looked out the window. Despite analyzing the miscellaneous building supplies spread around the gaping holes, I hadn't been able to figure out what they were doing. It was too soon to predict what the complex would look like in the end. Like my life in Hong Kong, I couldn't tell what the changes would bring.

My childhood friend Kaylee visited me in Hong Kong in April. We had been friends since we were classmates in a one-day-a-week homeschooling program. We stayed in touch when I went to a full-time high school and then when I went away to college. Kaylee shares my passion for literature, and manages to be both soulful and intellectual. She has a bright-eyed, positive attitude toward life that I've always admired. I was excited when she decided to visit me in Hong Kong—her first trip to Asia.

We took the iconic Peak Tram up to Victoria Peak on her second afternoon in the city. The rumbling funicular pulled us up the hill, giving eye-level views of the windows on the 40th and 50th floors of the skyscrapers. The tram carried us through the thick green jungle, rising into the clouds. After filling our cameras with the sprawling urban landscape, the tangled greenery and the light flashing off the sea, we sat in a café at the top of the mountain and shared a brownie. My armchair by a wall of windows overlooked the sweeping Hong Kong skyline.

"So, do you want to move to Hong Kong yet?" I asked.

Kaylee laughed. "It's tempting, but I'd spend too much money shopping here."

"I know! But you should add it to your list of options."

"I don't know what I'm going to do," Kaylee sighed. Just off of six months teaching English in Colombia, she was contemplating a move to China, where she'd found a potential teaching opportunity. She was in a state of limbo, a holding pattern. "I have even less direction now than when I was a teenager!" she said.

"At least you're not the only one."

"That's the problem with our generation," Kaylee said. "We spend all this time in college not growing up, and then we graduate and don't really know what to do—but we're not supposed to be *too* responsible or start families too young in this day and age."

"I think they call it extended adolescence," I said. It was true. I knew people older than me who were still undergraduates. They were in no hurry to finish college and rush into responsibilities. More, however, wanted responsibilities and couldn't find them.

"But it's a lot harder for us to find jobs than it used to be, too. It's so different than we expected," Kaylee said. The millennial generation faced a world that had changed very quickly. We were children in the '90s, a time of economic prosperity. We grew up as the internet exploded all over the world. We had been taught we could do anything and be anything if we only believed in ourselves. I'd always been confident that I could do whatever I set my mind to. That was why I decided to attend a college that put me $80,000 in debt. Of course I'd be able to find a job afterwards!

But our generation witnessed the fall of the Twin Towers in our formative years, and everything else started to shift and fall. We finished college and were trying to start our careers in the middle of global meltdown. We'd known a world that seemed darker and more difficult than the Gen X-ers experienced before us. As our governments descended deeper and deeper into debt, we were living with the consequences of another generation's mistakes. We were less confident that we would be able to do all the things we were told we could do as little kids.

Among my own group of college friends, only a handful of people stayed in New York after graduation. The rest moved in with their parents or took jobs around the globe. We were looking overseas for career opportunities. We didn't want to be insulated in picture-perfect America because it wasn't picture-perfect anymore. We were not convinced by the previous generations who taught us that ours was the best country in the world. It was becoming increasingly clear that the time to live abroad was now. We were becoming the global generation.

"What would you do if you stayed in Arizona?" I asked Kaylee.

"I'm not sure. There isn't as much of a place for me. Everyone in Gilbert is either still in school or they're a couple with kids."

"You should move to Hong Kong. This is where things are happening." I pulled out my camera as the Peak Tram pulled up the hill, visible past Kaylee's elbow. "I know I don't fit in Gilbert." The tram passed beneath us with its cargo of tourists.

"You're always going off places. New York... London... now Hong Kong."

"I just don't want to be one of those women who keeps saying they wish they had lived abroad in their twenties." I set my camera back on the table.

"I hear that, too," Kaylee said, "but people I trust have also been counseling me to think about the relationships I've built in Gilbert. I don't want to abandon those... I just don't know." She took a sip of her coffee and scooted the rest of the brownie over to me.

"Maybe you can ease into the idea of China while you're here. I think you should go for it," I said.

"I figured you would," Kaylee said, setting her coffee cup back on the table. "It's nice to think about it away from home. I always agonize over big decisions." I thought back to the moment I decided to move to Hong Kong. The process was never agonizing. Ben was there. The decision was made. Even now, I believed it was the right choice.

When we returned to my apartment, I noticed that the holes in the courtyard had been filled in. Something had changed underneath the surface.

That weekend, Kaylee and I decided to partake of one of the bastions of old colonial history in Hong Kong: high tea at the Peninsula Hotel. We got dressed up and arrived at the Peninsula just after 3:30 on a Sunday afternoon. Potted palm trees and gilded ceilings decked the massive lobby. Square tables covered in teacups and trays of scones filled the spaces on both sides of the entrance.

"I wonder if we're supposed to go to the front desk," I said, doing my best not to look intimidated by the posh surroundings, or worse, to look like a tourist.

"Maybe we just take a seat? There are a few tables open," Kaylee replied.

"Hang on, is that the line?"

We found a sign advertising the afternoon tea from 3:00-6:30 p.m. A row of patrons stretched almost all the way to the side door of the hotel. We made our way past tourists and well-dressed ladies-who-lunch to the end of the line. "What do you think? Is it worth it?" I asked, counting the scores of people who had gotten there first.

"I don't mind waiting! We're already here."

We inched past high-end jewelry stores, leaning against cool marble as we waited for the tables to clear. We took turns holding our place in line and wandering around the hotel in search of the restrooms. The Peninsula's grand staircase led up to halls of designer stores and jewelry shops. We found the bathrooms behind Gucci, to the left of Tiffany's. The entire building felt like money, but money of an older variety. The kind that got dusty around the turn of the last century and never changed.

After 45 minutes in line, we sat down for the full colonial English experience. We ordered our choice of tea and shared a three-tiered platter of little sandwiches, scones and cakes. The tea came in silver pots and we drank from pretty china teacups. The snacks were sweet and decadent. The scones, clotted cream and jam brought me straight back to my student days in England when I had my first high tea at a little teahouse in Stratford-upon-Avon. We marveled at our surroundings and talked about Jane Austen and the Bronte sisters. Kaylee was a fellow English literature major, so we had plenty to discuss. "It doesn't feel like we're in Asia anymore," she said. I had the same thought every once in a while in Hong Kong. Then something very 'Chinese' would happen and I would remember how unique this place was.

"I've heard the Peninsula used to be 'it' for the people who came over from England, even people who couldn't afford tea in a fancy hotel back home. In Hong Kong they automatically moved up a class or two."

"What do you mean?" Kaylee asked.

"Their money went further here, and any foreigner was part of the privileged class. People were even carried around in sedan chairs back then." I imagined the Hong Kong of black and white photos.

"I would have loved to see Hong Kong back then."

"It's weird, but even I'm a higher 'class' here than I would be at home. I'm just an English teacher, but I make a lot more than the annual household income of Hong Kong families. It's a city, so things are expensive, but the tax rate is low and I live much better here than I would as a teacher at home."

"If you work in publishing in London, you'll go back to being poor."

"Yes, I'd better enjoy it while it lasts. Have I told you I started paying off my student loans early?"

"No one does that back home."

"I know. It feels like borrowed prosperity though, like sooner or later this expat life is going to disappear in a puff of steam." I had never talked about money as much as I did these days. Hong Kong had done something to me. More telling was the fact that I had started to pay off my loans though. They were a constant source of anxiety, but two years after graduation, I was knocking them off one by one.

"Maybe I should move to Hong Kong after all," she said, laughing.

At the height of the British Empire there were thousands of British nationals working for the government in Hong Kong. They came as civil servants and businessmen, attracted by the cheap services and housing stipends. However, the region was not without tension between the colonists and the locals. Riots erupted in 1967 as pro-communist groups rose up against the British. The violence started as a labor dispute and escalated to widespread bombing as the rogue groups reacted to the Cultural Revolution across the border. The leftists were rooted out, however, and the British kept their grip on this increasingly valuable little island.

I read articles about how, as the 1997 Handover approached, expats lamented the loss of their oriental paradise. They worried that it was time to return to England, where they would have to pay taxes and do their own laundry. However, Hong Kong had not declined in the years since the Handover, as many feared it would. Now the money was coming from China as well as the West. Many expats decided to stay under the "One Country, Two Systems" policy. Now the population of Hong Kong consisted of about five percent foreigners.

I looked around the opulent lobby of the Peninsula Hotel; over half of the patrons were Chinese. This experience was still limited to people with disposable income, but it was not only for the colonists anymore. Caucasians sometimes still had an unfair advantage, but now it was far more important to speak fluent Mandarin, Cantonese and English. Westerners were not the only people with status, and as China opened up for business they had less of an edge than ever. But the hand of Beijing was growing heavier on Hong Kong, and no one knew what that would mean for the future. One of the real worries was that the freedom of the press and freedom of speech that Hong Kong people, both local and expat, had long enjoyed may be in jeopardy. The Hong Kongers I talked to were well aware of the dangers that China could bring.

Despite the concerns for the future, this place was turning out to be a very lucky draw for me.

30

SEVENS

The Golden Lotus is a famous Chinese novel that has been banned in China pretty much since it was written in the 1600s. In it, the main character is a woman whose husband cannot satisfy her sexual needs, so she pursues various men until she finally takes up with a man who is equally sexually energetic. Then she exhausts him and he dies. So basically, it's about sex. During Kaylee's visit, Regina invited us to watch the Beijing Dance Theatre's performance of *The Golden Lotus* with her friend Lucy. The ballet took out some of the side stories and characters of the novel, but left in the orgies and affairs.

After we had been thoroughly impressed by the provocative performance, we wandered into Wan Chai, Hong Kong's red light district, in search of a taxi. There we encountered another carnivalesque spectacle: the aftermath of the Rugby Sevens.

Men stumbled out of the open-fronted bars along Jaffe Road. Women teetered on heels, and pushed breasts against muscled arms. Booze-fueled laughter reverberated across the street, a notch too loud. The smell of beer was strong in the air. Cigarette smoke left a perpetual haze above the revelers.

The Sevens are like Spring Party Weekend or the equivalent held at many universities in the US. People from all over the world roll into Hong Kong to have a weekend-long party. Ostensibly this is for a big rugby tournament, but it ends up being one huge celebration with non-stop drinking, wearing of costumes and—for some—a lot of sex.

"Lucy! How's it going!! Ahhh!!"

Someone wearing a pirate hat and an eye patch barreled into our companion on the street. The Sevens—for reasons I don't understand—gives people an excuse to dress up in costume like a springtime Halloween. They crowd the South Stand of the rugby stadium during the games like Comic Con rejects. The happy pirate tried to drag Lucy across the road to the pub on the corner. "You've got to come out with us!"

"I'm not dressed for it—I've just been to the ballet—I'm going out tomorrow night and I don't have the stamina for two nights of this!" Lucy wailed.

"Come on, come on! You have to come!" said the pirate. Her friends were already on their way to the next bar.

"I don't know, I don't know…"

Regina held her back. "You're going out tomorrow night and you still want to have a good time then, right?"

"I know, it's just so easy to get sucked in," Lucy said as she wistfully watched her friend diving back into the crowd on the opposite side of the road. "There's a guy dressed like a matador over there."

"We need to find a taxi." We wandered further down the street into the tumult. The busiest bar street of Wan Chai was not the best place to catch a ride during Sevens weekend. We watched people laugh and stumble all over the street. The high-income crowd was literally overflowing from the more expensive bars; students crowded the street corner outside 7-Eleven holding cheap beers in each hand. The elaborate costumes showed the level of dedication people had for this most serious of Hong Kong party weekends. "There's a pair of foxes. That's cute."

"I see a smurf."

"Check out the guy with the red, white and blue pants. He's dressed like an American." Having just been to the ballet, our demure pumps and black dresses didn't really fit in. We finally hailed a taxi. We piled in and drove along the busy street, slowing to avoid the stumblers and the shriekers.

"What a madhouse. Look at that mask!"

"Why are there so many people dressed as pirates?"

We left the crowds behind for the quieter reaches of Mid-levels. We dropped off Lucy ("I'm going to have such a crazy time tomorrow!") and wound back down the slopes of the Peak.

"What's your impression of Hong Kong so far?" Regina asked Kaylee as the taxi whipped around corners.

"It's kind of Disney-esque."

"Really?" I said, thinking of the debauchery we had just left behind us.

"I never would have thought of it like that," said Regina. "What do you mean?"

"It doesn't seem real. It's like all the cultures of the world have been brought together in one place, like the Magic Kingdom," said Kaylee.

"Except that this is the real deal?"

The taxi slowed as we drove through Lan Kwai Fong. The party people here wore expensive nightclub attire, laughing and squealing as they lurched through the streets. "Looking at these skyscrapers," Kaylee said, "and all these impeccably dressed people, it still doesn't feel quite like a real place—plus we've just seen all these costumes..." she laughed. I looked around and couldn't believe that I was still here. Hong Kong had a magic about it that made me feel I was part of something. Maybe it was like Disneyland. In seeing it through a newcomer's eyes, I realized how much I'd come to like it.

"If Hong Kong was a color what would it be?" Kaylee asked Regina and me as the taxi slowed down in the busyness of Lan Kwai Fong.

"Red," we both said at the same time. "Definitely red."

"Really?" said Kaylee, "I thought of it as more of a dove gray, like the color of the buildings and streets."

"No, Hong Kong definitely isn't gray," said Regina.

"Yeah," I agreed, "It's more of a red with hints of electric blue. I think of China as a red country, but Hong Kong is red in a rich, vibrant, energetic sort of way. China is a bit more austere. The electric blue is the city lights and the futuristic vibe of the city."

We cleared the crowds of LKF and drove past the busy late-night pizza place, my friendly neighborhood electronics store all boarded up for the night, and a darkened row of boutique clothing stores. When we reached Café Siam, the Thai curry place near the escalator, I said, "*Ni-do mhgoy,*" (right here, please) to the taxi driver and we said bye to Regina. By the time we took the elevator up to my apartment I was sure Kaylee was completely enchanted by my city too.

31

WEDDED

I was circling around the narrow space in my apartment when I heard Ben's words: "I won't be able to come in May."

"What?"

"You'll be working anyway and it's probably not the best use of my holiday time."

"I thought you were planning to visit?" He was about to switch to a new department for the final six months of his contract, and I was getting ready to buy a ticket to visit Bali at the end of the school year. But I'd been expecting to see him that spring.

"It doesn't make sense for me to come all the way there if you won't get to spend any time with me. I'd just be sitting around while you're at work. It's best if I don't take time off right when they're making their hiring decisions."

"But it's been almost three months," I said. I had been experiencing the itching that grew in the pit of my stomach each time I was away from Ben for too long. Missing him was a physical sensation, as well as a mental one. I had consoled myself with the hope that he would spend a week in Hong Kong in May.

"You know, I arrange to spend all of my holidays with you," Ben said, "but you are going to your sister's wedding during Easter and then off to Bali. I work quite hard and I don't want to make an extra trip if I can't spend any time with you."

"Wait a minute. I asked if you minded me going to the wedding. It was your choice not to come to that. As for Bali, you said you couldn't take too much time off at once, so I might as well spend some of my holiday doing something cool, since I have so much more time off than you." During our three-year relationship we had managed to see each other every three months, but it was becoming more difficult. "You said we'd see each other more this year, not less. After you found out about London you said you'd be able to take longer trips to Hong Kong and work in the Hong Kong office sometimes."

"I'm sorry, Shannon… It hasn't worked out like that. We'll just have to plan for a big holiday this summer instead." He sounded tired.

I wanted to cry. "What about June? I'll have a few days off for the Dragon Boat Festival, and you might know if you'll have a job offer by then."

"That might work. I need to go now, Shannon. We'll talk about it later."

I heard the phone click.

The pressure was building. I knew we couldn't sustain this long distance situation forever, but it felt like spending time together was no longer a priority. I worried that we were *too* okay with not being together too often. Did that mean we weren't right for each other? Were we *too* happy being independent and apart?

My friend Sam was also distraught. Eddie was returning to Canada to take a few classes toward finishing his degree. She would not see him again until their wedding that summer. "I don't know what I'm going to do without him," she said. "We spent two weeks apart when I got to Hong Kong before him and it was awful. I'm going to eat so much ice cream!"

I had never been like that. Priding myself on being in control of my emotions, I had always thought my ability to deal with my extreme long distance relationship was an asset. I usually felt so confident. Yet now I was upset to the point of tears. Ben was making yet another rational decision. He needed to get a job when his contract ended. He needed to show them he was serious. But why were we working so hard to be together if he could give up even our little bits of time together so easily?

The Easter vacation could not come soon enough. I was battling a roller coaster of emotions I wasn't used to, swept up in the motion of Hong Kong and the emotion of too much time apart. Fortunately, I was going home for Chelsea and Francois's second wedding. From the minute I hit the tarmac in Phoenix, I was allowed to be distracted by full-blown wedding prep.

Chelsea and Francois would be married in my parents' backyard. Chelsea was the oldest of the nine kids in my family—and the first to get married. In addition to the nine of us and various friends, a bunch of extended family came from Oregon and Colorado to celebrate with us. As soon as we picked them up from the airport they said, "What can we do to help?" and got right to work.

In between painting the pool fence and assembling centerpieces, I spoke to my grandparents about Hong Kong. They reminisced about the American Club, Repulse Bay, their home on Headland Road and their little Chinese junk. We compared notes about the places they had visited in Asia. One of the most fascinating stories was about when they went to a wedding among the boat people, also called the Tanka. Later, I found my grandma's account of the adventure in her letters:

One event which we found to be especially interesting was a Chinese wedding party we attended early in the year. We have been invited to many wedding parties and each has been a gay and happy affair. This one, however, was special for us, not only because it was unlike the others, but because it was the final celebration of the wedding of our boat boy, Santo. As we learned, a marriage of the boat people is totally different than that of any other class of Chinese people. We felt especially fortunate when we were told that it is very seldom a Westerner is in on such an event.

First of all, perhaps it would be well to say a few words about Santo. His name, actually, is Saam-gun, "saam" meaning three, and "gun" being a carry, a measure of weight. The literal translation, then, is 4 ½ pounds or his weight at birth! "Santo" is a name he has been given by the American bachelor business man he has been working for as a houseboy for several years. He is about 21 years old, a nice-looking young fellow, quiet and likable. He was born and raised on a junk and has lived under conditions most of us can't even picture. Yet, because he is a houseboy and boat boy for Americans, his status has skyrocketed. His marriage was one of the most talked-of of the year among the boat people of Aberdeen.

The dinner party took place on an old, decrepit floating restaurant in Aberdeen and was catered by Tai Pak, one of the new, elaborate floating restaurants nearby. We went by sampan to the flag-bedecked Sea Dragon, the large pleasure junk built by Santo's employer. We were appropriately welcomed here before boarding the restaurant. Our first act, after stepping onto the restaurant-boat, was to sign our names with a Chinese brush on the red satin souvenir cloth. Then, we greeted the bride. She turned out to be a very lovely girl in traditional black mandarin jacket thickly embroidered with silver dragons and other designs, and a red embroidered skirt (we were surprised to notice the skirt was worn over slacks, probably to facilitate climbing from boat to boat). She was nicely made up – powder, lipstick, rouge – and wore a red cloth flower in her hair. She had on a beautiful wide gold bracelet and wore two gold rings on her right hand besides her wedding band. These pieces of jewelry represented her total personal wealth at the time of her wedding.

Chelsea and Francois got married the same weekend as Prince William and Kate Middleton. It was an unusually windy day in Arizona, but the skies were a perfect turquoise blue. The guests sat on white folding chairs in front of two big trees in our backyard. A curtain of brightly-colored fabric strips hung from the trees, creating a fluttering, tropical backdrop. Chelsea looked amazing in her Hong Kong dress. Her blonde hair covered her shoulders in thick curls beneath the silver-edged veil. She walked across the makeshift aisle, our back patio, and had eyes only for Francois, in his TST-tailored suit. I thought about my own gown back at my apartment in Hong Kong. Ben had laughed when I told him about it, good-humored as always. I wondered when I'd actually have a chance to wear it.

Santo looked very handsome in a black suit with the red bridegroom's ribbon on his lapel. The dress of the bride, Santo, and the "best man" stood in direct contrast with that of the guests, other than the several Westerners present. Everyone else wore the only clothes they had, the everyday outfits of the fisherfolk. We congratulated Santo's grandma, a wrinkled little old lady with tiny eyes. There were all types of people looking on, as curious to see us as we, them. There were babies strapped on backs, some asleep, some crying, some indifferent. One boy, about 10 years old with a child on his back, could barely keep his eyes open. We learned that the wedding ceremony had been going on for two days and nights and that even the children had had little sleep.

Chelsea's reception also took place in the backyard beneath the two spreading trees. The tables were set with runners in brilliant tropical colors and arrangements of candles, mirrors, sea glass and smooth stones. Tables spread with a casual feast lined the outer edge of the pool area. The bar was tucked inside the pool gates. We'd made a sign with boards going in different directions, pointing toward the places where Chelsea and Francois had spent time together: South Korea: 5,394 miles, South Africa: 9,598 miles, Hong Kong: 7,546 miles. As the guests walked back and forth to the dessert tables, my brother Alex's band provided raucous entertainment. Grandpa wore a barong from the Philippines and smiled through his mustache. Grandma beamed at her family around her.

We noticed several older women in common black Chinese outfits with thin gold charms in chains about their necks. They had been engaged for the wedding and were the only "officiators" or authorities on how things were to be done in the correct tradition of the boat people. They, themselves, had been married years before as the customs dictated, which therefore qualified them to pass down from memory to this young couple the various acts that make up such a wedding. The charms they wore were gifts from the groom. About the room were hung a bedspread, a blanket, and two large black cloths which pinned to them were large Chinese characters cut of gold, silver and red paper. But however poor the surroundings and the people, we sat down to one of the richest banquets we had ever experienced in Chinese fashion. We were served ten delicious courses, consisting of every conceivable seafood, plus chicken, pork and beef dishes. We ate 'till we could eat no more. Santo and his bride sat with us until the meal was over and then very politely and shyly asked our permission to leave. After hearing of some of the things that had transpired during the two days and nights of traditional ceremony, we wondered why they had not already collapsed from exhaustion.

We have recently learned that the marriage of this young couple is a successful one, for they are expecting their first child very soon. If this first child is a boy, everyone concerned will be overjoyed. The feeling of the Chinese has not changed much throughout the centuries concerning the good fortune of having a boy child. (1961)

At the end of the night, before Alex's band played the last song, a police officer dropped in to let us know that the neighbors had complained about the noise. It was still before midnight—and we were packing up anyway. Everyone agreed that no party worth having is *not* broken up by the noise police. As the guests trickled away to their hotels, homes and after parties, the whole family helped clean up the aftermath of emptied dessert plates and beer bottles. We folded red, orange and yellow table runners and packaged up leftover food that would feed the remaining house guests over the next few days. My youngest sister, Kylie, collapsed onto the couch in bare feet and a pink dress and sighed, "I love weddings."

We were a family that relished traveling off to exotic places, but it was good to be home.

I had jumped right back into the family routine that week, but something was different. My brothers and sisters were becoming teenagers and young adults, changing quickly as they grew taller than me. They all seemed so close to each other, with private jokes and grown-up banter— but I was drifting further away. It felt good, for a moment, to be a part of what I had given up by following Ben abroad. I wished he had come home with me for this.

32

FULL CIRCLE

Back in Hong Kong, the students were happy to see me, the teachers smiled, and I still felt exhilarated when I walked beneath the skyscrapers. I was being invited to more junk trips, more dinners, more afternoon coffees. My loneliness finally felt like a thing of the past. Now I just wanted the difficulties of my love life to be a thing of the past too.

Another Saturday found me on another bus to Sai Kung for a junk trip. The day had dawned cloudy and misty, but I packed my swimsuit and sunscreen anyway. We drove straight to the waterfront, lined with ice cream stands and street hawkers. Fishing boats and yachts bobbed, side by side, in the water. Families and couples strolled along the boardwalk, jostled by the fishermen going about their business. The air had the sharp tang of salt and rain.

I joined Samantha, Regina and Catherine, and Shane and Lauren, the Canadian NETs that I met on our induction course, at the docks. Our vessel waited, looking like the love child of a cruise ship and a regular junk. This was the biggest party boat in Hong Kong, capable of carrying a hundred people. A speed boat, banana boat and various floating water toys accompanied it. Rumor had it there was a karaoke lounge aboard. I couldn't feel the boat moving at all when I crossed the gap between deck and pier. Up three flights of stairs, on the top deck, we settled into chairs and benches in a corner. A European crowd, mostly members of the expatriate networking group Internations, which had organized the excursion, filled the lounge chairs and benches around the boat.

We ate chips, drank makeshift mimosas and talked shop: "I have a student named Wintry. Do you have any weird student names?"

"Oh yeah, I have a boy called Smile and a girl named Circle," I said.

"We have two teachers with the English name Fanny," said Sam.

"That's a little awkward," said Catherine. She's British, and fanny means something different in the UK than it does in the US...

"Old-fashioned names seem really common here," Regina said as she poured another glass of orange juice into her champagne. "I have a Lois, an Ella and a Shirley. We have about six Helens."

The crowd on the boat was friendly, but the weather was not. Before anyone in our group had a chance to change into swimsuits, it was raining. We watched as clouds rolled across the sky and a veil of water fell over the little islands around us. "Who's up for karaoke?" Sam said.

"Oh me! Definitely." Catherine waved both hands. Despite my deep and abiding fear of karaoke, I followed them into the depths of the boat, careful not to slip on the wet deck. We found our way to the bottom level where, beneath a shifting disco ball, a young woman danced alone on a tiny dance floor, watching her image projected onto a TV screen by a camera embedded in the roof. We left her to it and walked past an empty bar to a sitting area complete with a bizarre assortment of photos on the wall and a big-screen karaoke machine. Sam pulled out the microphone and filled the room with her powerful soprano. We spent the next hour singing karaoke (I listened and only joined in on group songs) as the rain poured outside. A pair of German girls joined us. Then a French guy. A girl from the Mainland. Sam spoke tearfully of Eddie, who was still studying in Canada. She sang "Leaving on a Jet Plane" and downed another beer.

I separated the mic from my fingers and stepped out of the little door to the narrow deck running around the outside of the boat. I leaned on the railing and watched the sheets of rain nearly obscure the little islands. In the foreground, a few guys had commandeered a floating raft. The rain came down, pattering into their open cans of Heineken. Music played behind me and laughter filtered down from the top deck. There was a stillness about the rain. I was dry and comfortable beneath the dripping awning. I thought about how strange it was to be lost on the other side of the globe, surrounded by other wandering souls. I probably wouldn't see most of these people again, but we shared a peculiar camaraderie because we were all far from home. The rain sifted the sounds of merry-making around me.

"Look out!" I had a brief impression of lime-green swimming trunks and a pale, skinny back before a splash erupted in the water. I stepped back before the second suited swimmer catapulted from the deck above me.

"Oi! You coward!" The guy in the water shouted. I sensed a moment's hesitation before a third body dropped from the deck with less grace than his friends. The guys in the water roared with laughter as their friend surfaced.

"I just wanted to give you guys a chance to clear out," he said, face scarlet.

"You should come in too!" one of the guys shouted at me. "There's nothin' like swimming in the rain!"

I smiled and waved, but declined the offer. I was happy with my solitude in the midst of this crowd for the time being. As the rain eased up, I glanced around and took stock. I didn't recognize myself. Who was this worldly person on a big party boat in the middle of the South China Sea?

After a rainy spring, June dawned sunny and hot. Tourists carried guidebooks around the streets. Many appeared to be from Mainland China. Like a true local, I found myself getting annoyed by people stopping on the streets to take pictures, interrupting the flow of the city. They wandered in noisy tour groups and walked very slowly. However, I felt a rush of pride when a Chinese woman stopped me on the street and asked me for directions to a famous Chinese restaurant. I felt even more proud because I knew where it was.

One morning on the long walk to school, I recognized someone. "Hello. I talked to you once before," he said. It was the grandfatherly man who spoke English with me on one of my very first lunch outings.

"Hello! I remember you." I smiled.

"It's nice to see you again," he said.

"Nice to see you, too." He nodded politely and walked on. I saw him the next day and we wished each other good morning again. The day after that he tipped his safari hat as he walked past. I felt like such a regular.

The final exams were approaching, so my classes were suspended again to allow for extra review time. I was to spend the entire month of June and the two weeks of school that stretched into July with few responsibilities. I cleaned the English room, organized my lesson plans and resources, and dreamed of the summer.

We had one final English Day in June. English Day was the time each month when the students got an extra push to use English outside of the classroom. There were two target questions for each month, and a group of older students called the English Ambassadors gave the little ones stamps on pink pieces of paper for each English question they answered. My friend Anthony wandered the playground with his stamp balanced on his clipboard.

On the days leading up to an English Day, I always stood out front with a big whiteboard that said, "Today is English Day!" and cajoled passing students to speak English. On the morning of the June English Day, Helen stood with me as I chatted with the students and asked them the target English questions for that month.

"What place do you like?"

"I like Ocean Park!"

"I like the school library."

"I like Ocean Park!"

"I like Hong Kong."

"I like Ocean Park!"

My friend Choi Sze Hin came over as usual, with his signature smile.

"Good morning Miss Young!"

"Good morning! Today is English Day!" I said.

"Yes! English Day!" He smiled.

"What place do you like?" I asked. He looked at me, then at Helen, and then glanced at the whiteboard.

"I like Hong Kong!" he said.

"Very good. What activity do you like?"

"I like badminton!" he said after perusing the list of activities I'd written on the whiteboard.

"Very good. See you later!"

"Bye bye! See you later!" He skipped off to the staircase, his blue backpack bouncing from his shoulders.

"Does he talk to you every day?" Helen asked as we watched him go.

"Yes, he usually waits by the lift after lunch."

"He is a good boy," she said. "His English has improved a lot. His pronunciation is better than some of the teachers!"

"That's all because of him. He's the one who makes the effort to talk to me every day."

Choi Sze Hin had no fear. When the other students were timid, when the teachers were insecure, when I was shy—he was the one who made the effort to connect. If I moved to another country again—whether it be to the UK with Ben or to Timbuktu—I would want to be more like Choi Sze Hin.

One ordinary day in June, Mr. Liu called me by my first name. Actually he called me Sharon, but it was still a major milestone. The next morning, he smiled and said good morning as I passed him with my teacup on the way to my desk. A week later, he asked me which of two English phrases was more correct. Then he waved goodbye as I left for the day. Somehow, something had changed.

I was glad I was living in Hong Kong instead of just traveling through. I had been in the country long enough to adjust to people's idiosyncrasies and get to know them. Maybe I was even earning their respect.

When final exam week began, Flora waited for me each day so she could accompany me to lunch. She would wave and call my name, bouncing on the balls of her feet and smiling through her spectacles. To save time, we went to the restaurant that was closest to our school. It was a typical *chah chaan tang* (tea restaurant) full of working men and parents who had just picked up their kids from school. The teachers called it *Ngoh Dak*, but it also had an English sign naming it Café Rendezvous. It was an incongruous label for such an unassuming noodle joint.

Ngoh Dak did not have an English menu. I went to lunch with the same group of teachers every day, and every day they explained the items on the set menu to me. I alternated between rice dishes with curry and vegetables and hot bowls of soup swimming with noodles. Fishing for noodles with chopsticks had become second nature. I had taken to bending low over my bowl like the local teachers to keep the soup from splashing my clothes.

The first time we went to *Ngoh Dak,* the waitress, who was the mother of one of our students, put four green plastic cups of warm water on the table. As she talked and laughed with the *louh si* (teachers), I took a few sips of my water. Then I glanced at the table next to us and noticed that the construction workers were washing their chopsticks in their green cups. Jenny had put a stack of chopsticks and soup spoons into one of our cups. No one else was drinking from them. I discreetly put my cup back on the table.

Each day I learned something new about my friends. The pictures I had formed of them after months of watching them laugh in the staffroom, shout at the students, and rush in and out of the elevator were being fleshed out. I learned more about their lives apart from school. Rita Pong had family in San Diego, and every time she went to visit them she brought back boxes of See's Candies because they were cheaper in the US. "Immigration is so difficult in USA," she said one day as we scarfed down rice and fried chicken in the *chah chaan tang*.

"Yes, it is."

"They always ask me so many questions. Last time they took my box of chocolate and searched me. I was alone, and they asked me these questions. It was so scary." Rita put down her chopsticks and took a sip of her iced lemon tea.

"They're not very friendly," I agreed.

"Yes, and you have to take off the shoes and they search everything," she said, shaking her head at American homeland security.

The last time I flew through Los Angeles, I had to stand in the new full-body X-ray machines. "Yeah, security gets worse all the time. It's not like Hong Kong, which is always so quick and convenient," I said. The papers had recently named Hong Kong International the best airport in the world for a second time. Security never took more than three minutes, and immigration was even faster if you had a Hong Kong ID card.

"Yes," said Rita, "I like USA but I think Hong Kong is better in this."

"Me too!"

It was nice to have something to talk about beyond food and our classes. I remained silent more often than not during the meals, comfortable sitting in the group and letting the teachers talk around and above me. I appreciated the company and didn't need to understand the conversations all the time. My experiences at the school were taking on a level of maturity. Everything was not as new and exciting as the early days of sweepstakes adventures, but I had found a place in spite of the language barriers.

33

TAIPEI

As I was riding the high of my new life, I couldn't wait for the coming Dragon Boat Festival weekend, when I would get to see Ben again. We would watch the boat races, perhaps eat sticky rice dumplings unwrapped from bamboo leaves; we would hunt for dragons together.

Then, with days remaining, Ben couldn't get the vacation time. The company still dallied over which trainees would get permanent positions. No one could risk taking time off.

When Ben called with the news, I felt the all-too-familiar sense of resignation at more thwarted time together. In May I had been upset. In June, I just felt cold. I was used to this. I sat on my wood floor, feeling the rough grains beneath my fingers.

Ben spoke, but his voice came from far away, much further than the thousands of miles separating us. He said he'd definitely have time off in the summer. We'd have answers by then. My phone was pressed tight to my ear, but his voice came through years of separation, miles of effort to be together. This would be the longest time we had ever gone without seeing each other: more than six months.

And what if he got the permanent job in London? Even for lawyers, jobs there were competitive, hard to find, but I had the sinking feeling that he was going to get it. At this point I wouldn't be surprised…

The tears finally came. The black pleather couch supported my back and afternoon light drifted in through my window. The ground shifted beneath me, unstable, angry. I rubbed a pattern of melting mascara across my face and listened to Ben's apologies, his reassurances.

When the reality settled in, I hung up the phone and booked a last-minute plane ticket to Taipei.

Sam and Emma had planned a fun girls' weekend, and now I didn't have anything keeping me in Hong Kong. I hadn't done any planning or research, but it dulled the pain of another postponed reunion.

Sam and Emma had booked their tickets for Saturday morning, but the only last-minute flights available were on Friday night. I walked the fifteen minutes from my front door to the Airport Express station, dropped off my luggage and picked up my boarding pass at the check-in desk conveniently located in Central. The train journey was only 25 minutes from Central, but I didn't even have to carry my luggage that far. Hong Kong was nothing if not convenient.

As the jet lifted off the runway in Hong Kong, I looked out the window and saw a fire dragon. It was painted large on the engine of the plane. Red light played over it as we rose through the clouds above the Mainland. A chill went through my body, unrelated to the aggressive air-conditioner above my seat.

What will I find in Taiwan? I wondered as the fire dragon and I descended through the black sky above Taipei's flat city lights. That island had been sundered from China six decades before. Free from the influence of Chairman Mao, it was a picture of what the Mainland could have been like. I had heard Taipei was a city that was not quite as advanced and global as Hong Kong. Was that because it had been left to its own devices without the British? Was it missing out on the grand Chinese wave of progress that was swelling underneath Hong Kong?

With the fire dragon still playing behind my eyelids, I entered the airport terminal. A small crowd of paparazzi was photographing a short, tanned man. His disheveled hair reminded me of Ben's when we first met in London, its Chinese characteristics making it stand on end. I tried to memorize his face, but had no idea who he was.

Minutes later, I was standing in a crowded bus line outside the terminal. The air was warm and fluorescent lights lit up the sidewalk as bright as day. An airport employee shouted instructions in Mandarin to the people in line. "TAIPEI TERMINAL?!" he shouted at me, and I held up my ticket. I was used to Chinese yelling by now, and his Mandarin was not nearly as intimidating as the harsher tones of Cantonese. He motioned me and a small Chinese woman beside me to the front of a new line.

"Are you going to the main bus terminal?" The girl asked as she pulled a heavy red suitcase up beside me.

"I think so. That's where I can get the MRT right?"

"Yes, that's where I am going, too," she said.

"Did you come in on the flight from Hong Kong?" I asked.

"Yes, I am from Hong Kong." She was silent for a moment, and then said, "I met Aaron Kwok on the plane!"

"Oh, um, I don't know who that is. I saw the guy with people taking pictures of him."

"Yes, that's Aaron Kwok. He's a big Hong Kong movie star. He's so good-looking!"

"Oh, I didn't realize that. He is good-looking." So many aspects of Hong Kong culture were still hidden behind the language.

"What do you do in Hong Kong?" she asked.

"I'm an English teacher."

"That's nice. Do you like to shop?" She was very well dressed. Like most Hong Kong women, she looked far trendier than I ever would.

"Sometimes. I've heard that Taipei has some good shopping too."

"Yes, I come here all the time to shop and see my friends."

The bus man shouted at the crowd as a bus lumbered up to the curb. The first line scrambled aboard and rumbled off to their destination. He shouted at us again.

"He says Taipei Main Station will be the next bus," the girl told me.

"Okay, thanks. So, you speak Mandarin and Cantonese?" Her English was better than I normally heard in Hong Kong.

"I speak Mandarin, Cantonese, English, Japanese and French," she told me.

"That's impressive." I tallied up my mediocre language abilities and came up far short of that: English, rusty high school German, mostly forgotten ancient Greek from college, broken and fractured Cantonese.

"I spent one year studying in France on a language exchange. Then I was in Japan to do another language course until the earthquake. I came home to Hong Kong after that." We talked about her job in Hong Kong working as a buyer for a fashion company. I had thought she was younger than me, but it sounded like she was firmly established in a stylish crowd in Hong Kong.

Our bus finally arrived and I thanked my new friend for pointing it out. I climbed aboard with my small bag as she heaved her big red suitcase into the compartment under the bus. My seat stuck in a reclining position. The curtains and faded brownish-orange interior were straight out of the seventies.

The bus pitched through the darkened streets and I got my first look at Taipei. The outer suburbs looked more like an older American city than they did like Hong Kong. I saw the usual assortment of Western and Chinese businesses, but it felt more familiar than Hong Kong. Most of the buildings were one or two stories tall, without the vertiginous density of Hong Kong.

I noticed other differences, like the occasional well-lit shop window with a scantily clad girl sitting on display inside. I had never seen that in Hong Kong. Prostitutes tended to roam the bars in Wan Chai and mingle with the revelers on the streets. These streets were empty and these girls looked fatally bored as they waited under the fluorescent lights for customers. I thought back to the Macau Fishbowl. (I would later learn that these sexily-dressed women in the shop windows were actually selling betel nut.)

Every so often we stopped to pick up or drop off passengers. This was going to be a longer ride than the 40 minutes advertised on the airport website. Eventually we crossed a bridge into the busy section of Taipei, where I saw more skyscrapers. There were more tall buildings than Phoenix has, but the numbers were still no match for Central, Hong Kong or Manhattan. By this time at night the streets were quiet, and the city felt empty. There were so few people standing around the bus and rail terminal when we finally arrived that I feared it had closed already.

A few tentative steps around the bus did not reveal any signs for the subway. I felt a stab of panic and realized I needed help. I would have to trust strangers in the middle of the night in this foreign city. The girl with the red suitcase was starting to walk away. I jogged over. "Excuse me, sorry, do you know where the entrance to the MRT is?"

"Um, I'm not sure, but it might be closed. You may need to take a bus." I did not relish finding my way to a strange bus in the middle of the night when I didn't have a clear idea of where everything was. I had decided to stay in a youth hostel on my first night, something that I hadn't done since college, in order to get the full solo traveler's experience. I had carefully written down directions from the airport bus to the MRT to the hostel. I did not plan for a closed MRT. Then my companion spoke again: "That guy over there is looking for the train too, maybe he can help you."

She waved over a tall Taiwanese man who looked like he was in his late 20s. "You are going to the MRT right? Maybe you can go together?" They spoke in Mandarin for a few minutes and took my piece of paper that had the name and address of my hostel. "Okay, his stop is close to yours, so you can find the MRT together. If it is closed you can share a taxi," she said.

"Okay, thank you so much! Have a good time in Taipei." As I followed this complete stranger into the nearly empty terminal building, it occurred to me that I didn't know the girl's name. She had already disappeared.

The young man introduced himself as Bao-Zhi as he guided me through the station. We were just in time for the very last train. Our bags banged against our backs as we sprinted through the train doors. We sat down on stiff orange seats and I asked my guide a little more about himself. He apologized repeatedly for his English, which sounded fine to me. I was surprised to learn that Bao-Zhi had just returned from a business trip to China. There was still tension between the two countries that the Mainland Chinese government claimed were one.

Eventually I bid farewell to Bao-Zhi and found my way out of the closing train station with his directions. I liked how brazen I was becoming in Asia, blindly following a stranger through a foreign city. It was becoming a matter of course to make new friends around the world. I walked down a deserted residential street to the hostel I'd booked just days before leaving Hong Kong. When Sam and Emma arrived, we'd be staying in a hotel, but it was fun to do this part of the trip alone. Shadows skittered between the short townhouses, and cats and bicycles punctuated my path. I felt brave as I reached the end of the dark lane. My keys were taped to the front door with a hand-drawn map to my dorm room. I let myself quietly into the little house, deposited my shoes in the pile by the door, and tried not to wake the two sleeping girls in the bunks next to mine. Half an hour after I arrived, two more girls appeared in the room. I listened to their French whispers while drifting off to sleep.

The next morning I scrambled into the shower before my housemates were awake, then packed up my things and waited in the little kitchen until the manager arrived to check me in and out of the hostel. I sat at a big wooden table and talked to the French girls, who were backpacking around Asia. Like me, they had chosen the hostel because it was cheap, and they wanted to meet other travelers. A map on the wall was stuck full of pins representing all the young people who had cycled through that room. I felt a thrill. I was one of those young people traveling the world, seeing where life would take me—even if I didn't usually travel with a backpack.

Eslite, Taipei's magical 24-hour bookstore, called to me that morning. Despite the early hour, it was packed with readers of all nationalities. The muted, fervent quiet of the bookstore made me feel at home. Later, the MRT brought me to the hotel where I would stay with Sam and Emma for the next two nights. I watched suited businessmen check in. A group of Japanese tourists filled the seats in the polished lobby, chattering happily.

One of my friends from university lived in Taipei with her parents and was planning to show Sam, Emma and me around the city. Lola squealed my name when she entered the hotel lobby. She looked more sophisticated than ever, fitting perfectly into the blend of cute, flirty and refined that so many Chinese women seemed to adopt naturally. We sat down for a coffee while we waited for the other two to arrive. It was hard to believe we were 8,000 miles and two years away from the little town in upstate New York where Colgate University is located. We caught up on our jobs and the people from school that we had seen in the last two years. We talked about Ben and the difficulties of long distance relationships. Lola had been in one for eight months with a boy from college, but the distance had made it too difficult for the relationship to last.

Lola was caught in the middle of cultures in Taipei, Chinese and American, even though both belonged to her. "It's tricky to find men that I can really talk to here. They're all either really immature or their English isn't good enough for us to really connect," she explained. Even in an international city, it was difficult to find someone who could meld with her blend of cultures. I was grateful that my Hong Kong guy, Ben, was such a brilliant communicator in English. But I was worried that words were not enough.

When Sam and Emma arrived, we embarked on two fabulous days of shopping, street food, sights and massages. Lola regularly entertained clients for work, so she was an expert at showing visitors around the city. We went to a huge monument to Chiang Kai-shek, the leader of the Republic of China who had founded modern Taiwan in 1949 after being exiled from the Mainland. Its huge open spaces bordered by elaborate traditional Chinese buildings reminded me of Tiananmen Square in Beijing. I was impressed by how much open space I saw in Taiwan, something that was no longer available on Hong Kong's densely populated island. It was surprisingly rare to see "Chinese"-looking buildings in Hong Kong. In Taipei we saw plenty of structures with big stone dragons, peaked red roofs and golden scrollwork.

Lola showed us the luxurious side of Taiwan, where services cost even less than they do in Hong Kong. We took taxis everywhere, went for foot massages, and had our hair washed and dried in a cheap salon. We watched the dragon boats race like insects across the river and ate copious amounts of food.

Taipei is famous for its busy, trendy night markets, and that was at the top of our list for the trip. Emma had arranged to meet up with one of her boyfriend's buddies from university on our first evening in Taipei. He had studied in Canada, but now he lived in Taiwan again, just like Lola. These young members of the Asian diasporas were returning to Asia to find work, just like me, just like Ben. He met us at the train station near the Shilin night market.

"Hi, you're Thomas right?" Emma said. She had never met him before, but she'd seen his picture on her boyfriend's Facebook page.

"Yes, hi. Hello ladies. Welcome to Taipei." Thomas was tall and clean-cut, and he seemed nervous about acting as tour guide for a group of girls he didn't know.

"So, did you girls bring any marijuana with you from Hong Kong?" Thomas asked, apparently to break the ice. We gave each other sidelong glances.

"Um, no we didn't."

"Oh, okay," he looked disappointed. "So who has been to Taipei before? Are you planning to do some partying here?"

"We're more interested in trying the street food... Heard it's really good," I said.

"Oh," he sighed.

We joined a throng of people crossing the road near the MRT station. Lola told us there were two sections of the market, one that was mostly food, and one that was mostly shopping. A few stalls of each mixed the sections together. The spaces between the stalls were starting to fill with young people. The smell of frying oil hung in the air.

"Look at that jewelry!" Sam gasped with her characteristic enthusiasm. We spent a few minutes milling around a table displaying very cheap earrings and an assortment of tangled necklaces that looked like candy strung across the table. The surrounding stalls had handbags, headbands and heels. The colors of the market were bright, cheap and cheery.

I picked up a few pieces, but soon realized that the styles were too cutesy for my taste. I followed my nose in the direction of a food stall and bought a little paper cup full of fried mushrooms. The smiling woman behind the deep fryer handed me a long toothpick. I stabbed a piece and brought it to my mouth. It was fresh and so hot that it burned my tongue. Eyes watering, I walked back to the jewelry table where Sam was still poring over the beaded wares. I sorted through the mushrooms with the toothpick, savoring each hot, greasy bite. The dough had been lightly seasoned and formed a shell that cracked in my mouth and released the fresh, steaming mushroom like a savory gift. It made me want to try every fried thing in the market.

Thomas made his way around the table toward me. "Where are you from?" he asked.

"Arizona in the US."

"Arizona! Is it easy to get marijuana in Arizona?"

"Um, I don't really know."

"Like, if you wanted to buy pot could you find someone to buy it from there?"

"Probably. I wouldn't know where to start." For all I knew, Arizona could be the easiest state in the country for marijuana.

"I was just wondering." He sounded disappointed again.

"What do you do, Thomas? Do you work in IT here?"

"Why? Do you think I am like a computer geek? Ha ha ha." His laugh was a little too exuberant.

I glanced at his preppy attire. "No, it just seems like there are lots of tech companies here. The only other person I've met from Taiwan worked in a computer company."

"No, no, I am not a computer geek. I am a teacher right now."

"Me too!" As we talked, I got the impression that Thomas was just a bit awkward. Perhaps he was trying to use pot references to break the ice with the Americans and Canadians.

We ate more fried things from the stalls and carts filling the market and eventually sat down at a greasy metal counter to order dinner. The family working behind the counter talked and laughed as they rushed back and forth, frying up the noodles and meat and vegetables. The smell of onions floated over the counter. They fixed our portions right in front of us and then scooted them towards us on bits of tin foil. We picked up the pieces straight from the grill with chopsticks, dipped them in bowls of rice and into our mouths.

After picking through the last shreds of noodles to retrieve the succulent bits of chicken, we collected our things and pushed through the crowds to the shopping section of the night market. We found stall after stall of cheap and trendy clothes, sunglasses, bags, toys and little gadgets. We bought gifts for friends back home and laughed at the lacy, frilly styles and tiny sizes. The styles favored by the locals in Taiwan and Hong Kong (and adopted by people like Sam) were very cutesy compared to styles in the US or Europe. There were baby doll dresses, frilly skirts, t-shirts for adults printed with Hello Kitty, My Melody (a bunny), Cinnamaroll (a puppy), and lots and lots of lace. Back in Hong Kong I usually relied on H&M for my clothes because they seemed slightly more grown-up than the usual market fare. I bought a frilly shirt for myself at the night market.

We kept losing members of our group in the press of people as each of us wandered off to get a closer look at something on display. The throng was made even denser by carts sitting in the middle of the street selling clothes and bags. "Those carts are illegal," Lola said. "They're not supposed to be here because they would make it too difficult for people to get out if there was a fire." As she spoke, a call went through the crowd and the vendor quickly folded up the racks of clothing sticking out of his cart and pushed it away down a side street, ignoring the people who had been perusing his wares. I looked down the street and saw that all of the extra carts had disappeared within seconds, leaving behind rapidly diminishing gaps in the crowd. A pair of uniformed policemen strolled through the street. They looked straight ahead, faces impassive. Minutes after the policemen had passed and melted into the mass further up the street, the carts pushed their way back into the middle of the road and opened for business again.

"Don't the policemen know the vendors do that?" I asked Lola as the illegal merchant leaned nonchalantly against his cart.

"Yes, but it's easier not to make a fuss about it. The vendors will find a way to get around the restriction. The police don't have to deal with what they don't see," she said. I watched carts appearing and disappearing from the middle of the crowded street half a dozen times that evening. The people in the swarm barely noticed. I couldn't imagine it happening in Hong Kong, where everyone seemed more controlled and law-abiding.

The next evening, we met up with Thomas again and he took us to a famous dumpling restaurant, Din Tai Fung. When the taxi pulled up to the curb, he bolted out of it and ran, arms flailing, to the door of the restaurant. We exchanged glances as we paid the fare and followed him to the door. "It is very crowded, so we have to put our names in as soon as possible," he explained. Inside, we found xiao long bao (I waited for it to cool this time), dumplings filled with sweet black sesame paste, and toilets that hosed off your backside.

After dinner we rode the high-speed elevator up to the top of Taipei 101, the second-tallest building in the world—for the moment. We finished the evening sitting on the steps outside another monument in the warm evening air.

I thought about how my visit to Taiwan compared to my visit to Korea months ago. At the time, I had barely known anyone, and had looked enviously at my sister's amity with her international friends. Eight months later, I was enjoying a girls' weekend and meeting up with people I knew all over the world. This was a chance I wouldn't have taken if Ben had been able to visit me that weekend. It threw into sharp relief the sacrifices I would have to make if Ben stayed in London. Over the last few months, my life had been rich with opportunities, revelations and the glorious possibilities of a life in Asia. As insects crawled across the pavement, the monument at our backs, I knew a terrible choice was coming.

34

Year's End

The evening before the last day of school, the teachers hung around for the end-of-the-year dinner long after the students left. I sat at my desk looking up activities in Bali, where I would be flying at the end of the week.

"Hey Shannon." The young classroom assistant, Chung, leaned on the edge of my cubicle. "How's it going?"

"Not bad."

"You going to the dinner tonight?"

"Yup," I said, already looking forward to the food. "Should be fun."

He snorted. "Maybe." Chinese dinners didn't hold the same novelty for him.

"Hey, I have a question for you," I said, glancing around the office. Helen and June were chatting by the hot water dispenser. "Do you know what happened to the last NET that was here? He only stayed for two months."

Chung had been at the school for less time than I had, but his aunt was one of the veteran teachers at the school. "Ohhhh… you don't know about that?" he said.

"No. Helen told me he went home because his mother was ill."

Chung glanced around too. We could see the tops of people's heads bent low behind the cubicle walls. Chung leaned closer. "He kind of went crazy."

"What?"

"My aunt was here. He came back to the staff room one day and he was shaking with anger. He threw a tray of food across the room and it hit my aunt—"

"What!" I nearly tipped over my mug of tea.

"I know! He pushed a pile of books off the desk and pulled down the window blinds. Then he stormed out and never came back!" Chung said.

"No way! No wonder everyone was so wary of me when I got here. What made him so mad?"

"The kids being naughty, I guess."

"I can't believe it! The kids are so sweet. Wow, I did not expect that." The pressure of culture shock could do strange things to people. I felt so sorry for my co-workers and the kids!

All of a sudden, Flora popped up behind me and said, "Miss Young! We go to play mahjong!"

"Right now? Okay." I hastily shut down my computer.

Miss Lo stuck her head over the top of her cubicle. "Sharon! You know how to play mahjong?"

"Nope," I said, "but I can learn." Everyone laughed and Miss Lo, Flora and I joined three other teachers who were making a break for the elevator. Some teachers were still working, but our group had decided that enough was enough. We strolled along the covered walkway to the private club where the end-of-the-year dinner was to take place. We were the first to arrive. The club had a large Chinese restaurant, a swimming pool, gym and various recreational activities for families. One of the Jordan Valley teachers was a member, so she had booked a small banquet room for our party. It had three large round tables, complete with lazy susans, two mahjong tables and the crown jewel…

"Karaoke!" shy Jenny exclaimed as we entered the room. "Miss Young! You like karaoke?"

"Ummmm," I stalled, but fortunately Flora started pulling out the ivory mahjong tiles, so I didn't have to answer.

"I will show you how to play!" she said. "You sit here and watch first." Flora, Miss Lo, Jenny and the other Flora sat around the square table and started mixing up the mahjong tiles. Mahjong is a traditional Chinese game that involves sets and patterns and families of tiles. I had seen people playing it before and listened to the telltale clacking of the tiles as I walked by mahjong schools in Wan Chai. Flora explained the basics of the game in her limited English. I promised to watch closely while the four of them played.

They arranged the tiles in smart lines, stacking them on top of each other to form a square pattern in the middle of the table, which was covered in green fabric like a pool table. They counted off fourteen stacks of tiles each and pulled them towards themselves, careful not to let anyone else see what they held. Each tile had tiny paintings of birds, flowers, circles, bamboo and Chinese characters.

"This one is the bamboo family, this one is the, how do you say, the ball family." Flora approximated the Chinese words that she had used to play this game for her entire life as she explained it in English for the first time. "This is north, south, east and west. This is the flower, it means you get another one." At this point I got lost in the flow of instructions.

"I'll just watch and try to catch on." I was mesmerized by the shifting of the tiles and the way the women's hands deftly moved each piece around until they had sets and pairs and families. I asked questions as they played and tried to guess what Flora would do each time it was her turn to select one of the cold, cubed tiles from the center of the table.

While we played, the other teachers started arriving from the school, happy to be finished with a year of intense work. The first group to join laughed out loud when they saw us. "Miss Young can play mahjong!" they screeched.

"I'm learning," I said. They turned from the table and made a beeline for the karaoke machine. Soon old Cantonese and Mandarin songs filled the air around the mahjong table, sung in time to the click of the tiles. The teachers were not shy about performing in front of everyone, and they asked me if I wanted to join in. I demurred, claiming that I had to focus on learning the game.

The energetic PE teacher—still wearing his shell necklace—laughed out loud when he saw me sitting at the mahjong table. "You play mahjong, la! Ha ha ha." I think he just found my existence amusing. He laughed at me whenever I tried to do Chinese things.

Helen and Miss Chan were the next teachers to arrive. "Miss Young can play mahjong!" they said. Helen beamed at me, and I thought I detected pride in her face as she looked at how well her NET teacher had assimilated into the group. I felt proud, but humbled at the same time. This group had welcomed me in, and seemed to love sharing their culture with me.

After watching a few rounds of energetic play, I asked if I could have a go. "Yes, you sit here. I can help you," said Flora. She sat by my shoulder like a little helpful bird, chirping instructions in my ear and patting me on the back every time I did something right. A few of the guesses I made about the way the game was played were completely wrong, but slowly I was finding my way.

When the principal entered the room, not long before dinner, he said, "Miss Young can play mahjong? Are you gambling?" I hadn't realized this game was being played for money.

"I'm just learning," I said, looking sheepishly at my friends around the table.

"They are a bad influence on you," Mr. Tsang said, but he too seemed happy to see me playing along with everyone else. We had in fact been playing for money. After the final round, I offered to chip in for our team because we lost spectacularly, but Flora insisted on paying up. Miss Lo beamed as she collected the cash.

We migrated over to the remaining spots at the big tables. I was seated right next to the principal, in the position of an honored guest, but this time I knew what to do. Using the serving chopsticks, I lifted noodles, fish, vegetables and spring rolls from the lazy susan into the waiting bowls of the people seated on either side of me. I tapped my fingers on the table in thanks each time my tea was refilled and listened closely to the Cantonese talk, sometimes even picking up the gist of the conversation. As usual, I tried at least a bite of everything on the table.

This was my first staff dinner with karaoke. I had heard rumors of karaoke at Chinese dinners, but thought it was more of a Japanese thing. I expected all the singing to take place after the meal was finished. I was wrong again. As soon as the first steaming plate of mushrooms and scallops arrived, the teachers started passing around the microphone and belting out Chinese classics from their seats at the table. They sang with abandon, mic in one hand and chopsticks in the other.

There were only five male teachers at the school, so anytime anyone selected a duet, the two men who were willing to sing got the job. One was kind-faced Mr. Choy who had been part of my lunch adventures since the beginning of the year. The other was a member of the maintenance staff, a huge man with a rolling accent that made his Cantonese sound different from everyone else's—even to my ear. He had a powerful, booming singing voice. Whenever it was his turn, he stood up and belted out his part of the song above everyone's heads.

"Do you know *American Pie?*" Principal Tsang asked me.

Silently, I was screaming, "No no no!" but I said, "Yes, that's a good song."

"I like that song too. I also like the Eagles," Mr. Tsang said as he put a few pieces of chicken into my bowl.

"I like them too. Have you ever seen them in concert?" I said, desperately trying to change the subject.

"I saw them at the Hong Kong Exhibition Center last year. It was great," Mr. Tsang said. Then he added, "If you can sing *American Pie*, I will sing with you." I was trapped.

When Don McLean crooned those first words, someone stuck the microphone into my hand. I practically whispered the words to the verses as my face turned from pink to a painful brick red. It's a difficult song under the best of circumstances. I hit half of the words at the wrong time. My only relief was that the screen was behind my seat so I didn't have to look at anyone. I panicked when it occurred to me that this was a famously long song, nearly choking on the lyrics. During the chorus, Mr. Tsang and I managed a respectable rendition of the words. Mercifully, the karaoke version of the song had been cut down to a manageable length, so I didn't have to suffer all the way to "the last train for the coast." I raised my voice for the final chorus and pitched it into the mic with a last gasp of gusto.

When we finished, all three tables erupted into cheers. "Miss Young! Miss Young!" my friends cried as I thrust the microphone away from me and tried not to cry myself. I buried my face in my bowl.

We finished dinner, and I felt as full and happy as I always did after a big Chinese meal. Everyone gathered for a staff picture and then wished each other happy summers as they began to disperse. Mr. Tsang offered Mr. Liu and me a ride because all three of us lived on Hong Kong Island. As we walked to the car, I made small talk, asking Mr. Liu about his summer break and whether he would return to the same school. He turned to me and said, "We hope you stay for one or two more years. It is difficult to find good NET teachers." I was speechless.

We drifted through the night in Mr. Tsang's SUV. I watched the lights of Hong Kong around us when we emerged on the other side of the cross-harbor tunnel. After all this time, the city still filled me with awe.

As the skyline flashed by, I identified as many buildings and streets as I could, thinking about the time I'd spent wandering those streets and staring at those lights.

When Mr. Tsang pulled the car to the side of the road in my neighborhood, I said, "Thank you so much for the ride. I really appreciate it." Mr. Tsang and Mr. Liu burst out laughing. I had no idea what was so funny. As they pulled away from the curb, I knew I still had a lot to learn about the people of Hong Kong.

35

LIMBO

One of the things uppermost in our minds at the present time is the fact that we are very soon due for our next 3-month leave. Though we as yet know no details and have made no plans, we expect to be winging our way homeward early next year. We do hope to see most of you then. You can be sure that we are excited at the prospects! At this point, we don't know whether we'll be returning to Hong Kong, or whether we'll be transferred elsewhere overseas. The suspense is great, and we are curious, admittedly. However, we do feel quite sure we'll be happy wherever we might go. (1961)

A rash of rainstorms and typhoons swung around the island, never quite scoring a direct hit. As the oppressive heat and pouring rain alternated each day, Ben waited to find out whether he would be offered a permanent job in London. His firm kept delaying and delaying. I didn't know what to feel anymore. Everything was in flux. The course of my life was in the hands of others. I had stopped paying attention to the old police complex outside my window. It hadn't changed in months, so I stopped watching it so closely for signs of transformation.

On the other side of the world, Chelsea and Francois were struggling too. Eager to get married and stay together no matter what, they hadn't planned their next step. They were finding it far more difficult to find jobs than they had expected. They were facing the possibility that they might need to spend some time in separate countries after all.

Ben and I chatted online every day, growing anxious as the summer approached. We spoke wistfully of the possible future, our conversations relegated to online messages.

Shannon: I would love to travel around Asia (or anywhere really)
             with you if London doesn't work out.
Ben: If I get a job here
             and I find out today
             can you just quit your job, fly over here and we can get
             married?
Shannon: Is that an offer?
Ben: Would you actually move?
Shannon: Well it seems like it would be prudent to finish out the
             school year.

I paused. I looked back at the words on my computer screen, feeling unsure.

Shannon: I think I would have to know that that's really what you
             want...
Ben: No time to be prudent when love is on the line.
             I really want you.

I stared at the blank space between my eyes and the screen. Would I really do it? After all of this long distance drama, would I really drop my new life in Hong Kong to start over again? A year ago, I had wished that Ben would just marry me when he found out about London in the first place so that we could be together as soon as possible. I thought I was ready to go then. Now, after all of this waiting and uncertainty, I wasn't ready after all. How could I tell him that? How could I say, "No, I want to keep working at a job that doesn't relate to my career aspirations in a country that is only temporarily mine"?

I said the only thing I could think of to say.

Shannon: I wish you were here.

I had to stay in Hong Kong.

I couldn't wait for a definite decision from Ben's firm. He needed to get the best job possible, but I needed to do what was best for me. I prayed that an opportunity would arise in Hong Kong, but if he got the job in London, I would embrace another stretch of long distance commitment. In the last year, Hong Kong had gotten into my soul and there was no turning back.

I bought a ticket to return to Hong Kong at the end of the summer break.

I got on the plane to Bali with no answers but this: I would be back.

What the future would hold for Ben and me, I didn't know.

We hadn't seen each other in over six months.

My friend Paige from university and Lola from Taiwan met me in Bali. We explored the beaches, temples and restaurants of the magical little island. As we basked in the sunshine and filled our stomachs with unfamiliar spices, I was distracted. I kept checking my email, waiting for some sort of news. Ben and I stayed in constant contact, but he didn't have any answers either.

We spent a few days by the beach and then a few days in the mountain town of Ubud. I borrowed Paige's phone to check my messages again. We went to see a traditional Balinese dance in the Water Palace. The dancing girls had painted eyes, tall headdresses and exquisite movements. They twisted their hands and held parts of their bodies perfectly still while the rest moved to the beat. My eyes filled with the colors and the glitter of gold leaf and brass gongs, but my mind was on Ben.

Along almost every street we saw shrines that looked like big mailboxes with long curved poles rising above them. At the ends of the poles, tassels made of bamboo leaves and flowers hung down over the streets. We asked one of our taxi drivers about them. "Those are the dragons for the Kuningan festival. You see they hang down like the necks of the dragon," he told us as he whipped around corners and weaved between skinny motorcycles.

Later, we joined a Balinese woman named Made who taught us to cook traditional Balinese dishes: chicken satay to dip in fresh peanut sauce that we had made using her stone mortar and pestle; banana leaves packed with tuna and spices and roasted over a grill; vegetables, spices and meat mixed and cooked and mixed and cooked again in ever more intricate and colorful concoctions. When we had filled ourselves until we couldn't possibly eat any more, we left the traditional family compound where Made lived with her husband, children, in-laws and domestic helpers. I looked back and saw that two stone dragons topped the gates of their home.

Dragons. No matter where I looked, I saw them. They represented how much I still had to discover about this strange and changing half of the world. They were burning, mysterious, intoxicating. Fire dragons. Whatever else would happen to me in limbo, I was caught by the mystery and romance of the dragons.

On one of our last evenings in Bali, Paige and Lola asked me to read aloud a few pieces of the document that would eventually become this book. I read the first few chapters, and they laughed and "awwed" at all the right places. They made sympathetic noises when I described the circumstances that had kept me so far away from Ben for so long. I wondered if this would be the end of the story. Our efforts to be together had been thwarted time after time. He was all I could think about as I sat there in a beautiful villa in the mountains, the spice-filled Balinese food still rumbling in my stomach.

When Paige and Lola were asleep, I walked out onto the terrace. The glow from the full moon shifted through the banana leaves and filled the valley beneath me. There was so much mystery, beauty and uncertainty in the world. I knew that if I had to be without Ben for a little longer than we planned, we would be okay. Things had already turned out to be better than my plans. I still had so much to discover on the far side of the world. I would continue getting to know Ben's home city, which had now become my own true love. If I was lucky, we would get to explore it together some day. Yes, we were still in limbo, but it wasn't such a bad place to be after all.

The morning after I sat on that moonlit terrace in Bali, I talked to Ben online. I was sitting in a wicker armchair as the morning sun streamed over my shoulder. My fingers shook as I tapped out messages of hope. It was our way of staying connected across the globe. And then he told me: the London positions had finally been announced. But Ben had been offered a job in Hong Kong.

In mid-August, I returned to Hong Kong. In October, barely a fortnight after my second Mid-Autumn Festival, Ben came home.

EPILOGUE

The fire dragon waited. It was surrounded by people and cameras and smoke. One by one, men in white shirts stuck long, thin sticks of incense into the twisted branches of the dragon's back. Bit by bit, the fire dragon grew. It glowed in the yellow light from the surrounding high-rises and in the deep, red light emanating from its spine.

I watched as the dragon bristled, built up for its entrance into the main festival. I had returned to Tai Hang for my second Mid-Autumn Festival, my second fire dragon. This time, I ventured further into the crowds and found the fire dragon down a back street. It was being created before my eyes, taking on light from the incense and energy from the gathering crowd.

This time, when the fire dragon barreled down the street and the dance began, I knew where it came from. I had seen it taking shape in the smoky alleyway, bit by bit, like the life I had built in Hong Kong. This time I knew what was coming. As the dragon danced, feeding off the energy of the spectators, I felt comfortable, proud. This was my place now, and I knew what to expect.

When the dance was over and the flames dispersed into the crowd, I held out my hand. One of the men walked straight to me and handed me three glowing sticks. I watched the orange tips fade to gray, and suddenly the magic of that night belonged to me in the form of three blackened pieces of incense. This fragment of Hong Kong was mine.

Author's Note

The events and conversations in this book are portrayed as accurately as possible, though some have been condensed and rearranged for pacing purposes. Most of the names have been changed to protect the privacy of my friends in Hong Kong. I am still here. One month ago, I left my little apartment above the old police compound—which is covered in bamboo scaffolding and change—and moved into a new flat with Ben. He is now my husband.

Shannon Young

Mid-Autumn, 2013

EXPLORE ASIA WITH BLACKSMITH BOOKS

From retailers around the world or from *www.blacksmithbooks.com*

learn that these sexily-dressed women in the shop windows were actually selling betel nut.)

Every so often we stopped to pick up or drop off passengers. This was going to be a longer ride than the 40 minutes advertised on the airport website. Eventually we crossed a bridge into the busy section of Taipei, where I saw more skyscrapers. There were more tall buildings than Phoenix has, but the numbers were still no match for Central, Hong Kong or Manhattan. By this time at night the streets were quiet, and the city felt empty. There were so few people standing around the bus and rail terminal when we finally arrived that I feared it had closed already.

A few tentative steps around the bus did not reveal any signs for the subway. I felt a stab of panic and realized I needed help. I would have to trust strangers in the middle of the night in this foreign city. The girl with the red suitcase was starting to walk away. I jogged over. "Excuse me, sorry, do you know where the entrance to the MRT is?"

"Um, I'm not sure, but it might be closed. You may need to take a bus." I did not relish finding my way to a strange bus in the middle of the night when I didn't have a clear idea of where everything was. I had decided to stay in a youth hostel on my first night, something that I hadn't done since college, in order to get the full solo traveler's experience. I had carefully written down directions from the airport bus to the MRT to the hostel. I did not plan for a closed MRT. Then my companion spoke again: "That guy over there is looking for the train too, maybe he can help you."

She waved over a tall Taiwanese man who looked like he was in his late 20s. "You are going to the MRT right? Maybe you can go together?" They spoke in Mandarin for a few minutes and took my piece of paper that had the name and address of my hostel. "Okay, his stop is close to yours, so you can find the MRT together. If it is closed you can share a taxi," she said.

"He says Taipei Main Station will be the next bus," the girl told me.

"Okay, thanks. So, you speak Mandarin and Cantonese?" Her English was better than I normally heard in Hong Kong.

"I speak Mandarin, Cantonese, English, Japanese and French," she told me.

"That's impressive." I tallied up my mediocre language abilities and came up far short of that: English, rusty high school German, mostly forgotten ancient Greek from college, broken and fractured Cantonese.

"I spent one year studying in France on a language exchange. Then I was in Japan to do another language course until the earthquake. I came home to Hong Kong after that." We talked about her job in Hong Kong working as a buyer for a fashion company. I had thought she was younger than me, but it sounded like she was firmly established in a stylish crowd in Hong Kong.

Our bus finally arrived and I thanked my new friend for pointing it out. I climbed aboard with my small bag as she heaved her big red suitcase into the compartment under the bus. My seat stuck in a reclining position. The curtains and faded brownish-orange interior were straight out of the seventies.

The bus pitched through the darkened streets and I got my first look at Taipei. The outer suburbs looked more like an older American city than they did like Hong Kong. I saw the usual assortment of Western and Chinese businesses, but it felt more familiar than Hong Kong. Most of the buildings were one or two stories tall, without the vertiginous density of Hong Kong.

I noticed other differences, like the occasional well-lit shop window with a scantily clad girl sitting on display inside. I had never seen that in Hong Kong. Prostitutes tended to roam the bars in Wan Chai and mingle with the revelers on the streets. These streets were empty and these girls looked fatally bored as they waited under the fluorescent lights for customers. I thought back to the Macau Fishbowl. (I would later